CHILDLESS BY CHOICE

The Joy of Not Having Children (P.S. Motherhood is Not for Everyone)

Neema Kisanga

DISCLAIMER: This book is intended neither to advocate nor dissuade individuals from choosing to bear or not to bear children in any circumstances. The decision of having or not having children is a significant responsibility and ultimately rests within the realm of individual discretion.

Published in Sweden

ISBN 978-91-988681-0-4

First Printing Edition, 2023

Table of Contents

Childless by Choice - The Joy of Not Having Children (P.S. Motherhood is Not for Everyone)

Table of Contents

LIST OF TABLES & FIGURES

INTRODUCTION

"That she bear children is not a woman's significance. But that she bear herself, that is her supreme and risky fate."

~ *D.H. Lawrence*

It's about time we had a conversation about the joy of being childless by choice because, for far too long, people have insisted on the fact that fulfilment can only be found in the eyes of our offspring. While that may have been true once upon a time (and is still true for some people today), we're far from living within the pages of your favourite fairy tale. In fact, life is pretty stressful at the moment and it's showing no signs of easing up. For most of us, keeping up with keeping ourselves alive is more than enough responsibility. We don't need – nor do we have a desire – to add young minds into that equation.

No, I'm not saying that the only reason why many of us are childless by choice is because we're stressed out and can't handle any more responsibility – although that does factor in. What I am saying, however, is that there are many reasons why someone might decide not to have children and these reasons are only becoming more compounded now.

Who is this Book For?

I'll be writing this book in a manner that directs most of the statements, questions, and insight toward people who don't understand the principle of being childless by choice. However, I will – from time to time – address those of you who have decided to march to the beat of that childless drum.

Why?

Well, I think it's important to bring those who do not understand the basic premise of being childless by choice into the conversation. If everyone is so tired of being asked why they aren't having children – and I know they are, then creating that understanding might just bridge the divide.

So, let's get back to the question.

Who is this book for?

This book is for anyone who is curious to know what it means to be childless by choice. Whether you're considering whether that is the right decision for you or you've already made the decision, this book will give you insight into why that may be the best choice for you. On the other hand, if you have anyone in your life who insists on asking "why" continuously, it might be easier to hand them this book than it is to sit down and try to explain yourself for the umpteenth time this year alone.

Ultimately, we're going to bring everyone in on the conversation so that we can begin moving forward as a courteous, more respectful, and caring society.

What Will We Discuss?

At this point, I've used the word "conversation" ad nauseum, so let's switch things up and go with "discussion" for now. You might be wondering what could possibly fill an entire book on the subject of the decision to be childless. The fact is that I could create an entire encyclopedic compendium on the subject.

But I won't do that.

Instead, I've taken the approach of writing this book from my perspective as someone who made the choice of being childless a long time ago.

We'll get candid about everything from how societal norms have turned into unnecessary pressure to antiquated stereotypes that pervade our own families. If you're ready to unpack how being childless by choice can be one of the best decisions a young woman – or young couple – can make, then let's dive in.

NEEMA KISANGA

Childless by Choice - The Joy of Not Having Children (P.S. Motherhood is Not for Everyone)

CHAPTER 1 – WHEN NORMS BECOME PRESSURE

“ *No bun in the oven yet?" "You two better get on to it soon or you'll miss your window." "You don't want to be that 70-something-year-old parent at school pickup." "If you don't find someone to settle down with soon, you're never going to be able to have kids." "Having children is the most selfless act in the world – they're the legacy you leave behind." "Who you raise is more important than what you do for a living."*

Should I keep going?

No?

Alright. Let's leave it there.

These are just a few of the comments that people (women in particular) get when they haven't had children by the time that society expects them to. The sad part of it all is that these comments don't come from random strangers, but the people closest to you. It's not like someone you don't know is just going to walk up to you on the street and say, "Tick tock – time to start making babies." No. They don't know you. They don't even know whether or not you have children. The unwitting (and sometimes knowingly) hurtful comments that aggravate, irritate, hurt, and annoy the childless person will always come from people that they know.

Now, I would be remiss if I left my earlier comment hanging. While it's more common for women to be on the receiving end of the stick with these comments, men get them too. Just think about it. How many times have you seen the following scene play out in pop culture – whether in movies, books, or series? The scene of a young man being berated by his mother usually goes along these lines:

"Son, I'm getting older. I've done everything for you throughout your life. Is it too much to ask for you to give me grandbabies?"

My point is that although it isn't as prevalent, men get asked these questions too and they become increasingly frequent with age as well as with the deepening of romantic relationships. It's almost as if we're expected to procreate simply because we're alive. Whether you're on the childless end of the spectrum, the hurtful slinging end of the scale, or somewhere happily in between, we need to discuss how pressurizing grown women (and men) has become the norm and why.

Normalcy vs. Unrealistic Expectations

Statistically speaking, women are still having children, so there's no need to worry that repopulating the earth will become a race to save humanity in the near future. However, studies show that women are waiting longer to have children and are having fewer children than previous generations. This, of course, will wane slightly with time – especially as women become increasingly more independent.

Yes. Gone are the days when women were expected to stay home and breed like rabbits while men went out to work and – in some cases – breed like rabbits elsewhere too. We're evolving and, as such, our desires are evolving with us. I want to make it clear that I'm not writing this book to sway anyone into not having children.

If that's something that you feel is right for you, then that's what you should do. Irrespective of what the world might seem like around you, if you want to have children, no one can stop you from having them. I'm not here to tell you when you should or shouldn't have children or whether it might be an irresponsible decision considering the recent spate of events around the world. I'm not here to play judge, juror, and executioner. However, I will be providing anyone who is considering not having children with as much information from both ends of the spectrum as possible. I'll also be providing that very same information to people who want to know more about the decisions of a friend, family member, or other loved one.

Why?

Well, if you really care about someone who has opted to not have children and you're just the curious type who wants to know why, then reading this book might give you a bit of insight. It sure will work out better than asking them!

Moving along.

As we look through the statistic looking glass, women are asked these questions more often for a number of reasons. For starters, we're seen as the life-givers of society. Our bodies are required for creating and incubating a human life. We're also, generally, more agreeable than men are and even other women will think that they'll get a more permissive or agreeable response from us. We also appear to be the gatekeepers of procreation and we, therefore, get these questions more often. Then there is the fact that society is so used to the idea of a barefoot and pregnant woman standing over a hot stove in the kitchen that anything to the contrary seems delusional.

There are some people, however, that are just completely oblivious that these questions are considered intrusive. In my experience, older generations and people who are firmly rooted in older belief systems – or societal norms – typically mean no harm when they pose these questions. To them, it's a matter of harmless small talk. In the same way that they might ask you how your day was or what the weather is like, the subject of when you'll be having children is not meant with any ill intent.

Keep in mind that, historically, women have been asked the question of when they'll have children repeatedly and it doesn't end when someone's had their firstborn either. After that, they'll be asked when they'll be giving their child a sibling. For those who have a second child, they'll be asked if they're done with their brood. It never ends and, for most people, standing their ground doesn't make much of a difference. While that isn't a blanket statement and it depends on who you're dealing with, there is some truth in the generalization. Just have a look at the table below to see why standing your ground can feel impossible – especially for young women.

Your relationship to the Questioner	Suggested Response	Exceptions to the Suggestion
Nuclear family member	Detailed discussion on not wanting to have children.	Toxic and narcissistic family members that will not hear you either way.
Childhood friend	Same as above but more candid in nature.	Toxic friends and those who are not close enough to you to warrant a deserved response.
Extended family member	Simple statement on the matter.	Out-of-towners that you do not have a close relationship with.
Someone in your work environment	Same as above but with less emotional attachment.	The office gossip or a person who is far too forward for a professional setting.

Table 1: The Types of People Who Ask When You'll Have Children - Knowing When to Engage.

In most settings, not engaging is more than sufficient. You shouldn't have to justify your reasons for anything. If you feel the need to answer a question once – maybe twice for the forgetful types – then go ahead and do that. However, if you feel like someone is prying or their words make you uncomfortable, it's perfectly fine for you to honour the feeling in your body and disengage from the conversation.

So, while men are statistically prodded on the subject of having children less than women are, we can't blame the patriarchal state of society or the more recently overused term, toxic masculinity, for the dilemma that we're faced with. In fact, there are times when I understand why people ask these questions simply because I've taken the time to understand the scientific premise behind certain elements of our collective status quo. There is a definite science behind the peer pressure that people insist on engaging in and it has a lot more to do with our primitive beginnings than one might think.

The Science Behind the Pressure

We, as human beings, like to think of themselves as creatures of logic. We want to believe that we've got everything under control at all times and that we're capable of using logic around the clock. For many people, embracing the fact that they are controlled, to some degree, by primitive instincts is unsettling, to say the least. In fact, it's downright offensive to some!

The reality is that whether you find it offensive to think that you're driven by your primal instincts or that you're not necessarily thinking rationally if you ask someone why they haven't had a baby yet, it doesn't change the fact. What do I mean by this?

Chapter 1

Well, let's take a walk down the proverbial memory lane of all humankind and go back to early humankind when practically all hominins lived in small family groups within the umbrella of their species. We, like all other Neanderthals, were no exception to the rule. [1] The reason why we formed these family units was for the sake of safety and efficiency. There was safety in numbers and having a member of the tribe who could stay in a safe space to protect the young of the group made procreation that much easier. But Neanderthals didn't have children for the sake of passing on a family name, having an honour-roll child to brag about around the watering hole, or having another (smaller) human in the mix to make the tribe a family. Instead, they had children so that they could pass on their genetics and, thus, keep their species alive. If you think about it logically, our survival instincts are no more special, important, or efficient than a virus. What's more is that the only reasons why female Neanderthals stayed back to look after children were:

- Males were typically larger, stronger, and faster than females, making them more adept at hunting.
- Females nursed their young for prolonged periods.

With all this in mind, be aware that it wasn't uncommon for the elderly (physically vulnerable) or the injured but not incapacitated (also physically vulnerable) to care for children while males went out to hunt and females foraged nearby. If this doesn't sound like your idea of an ideal life, then why would you cherry-pick the instinct that encourages you to bring another life into the world, but without the support structure that has historically been needed to rear that child?

What's worse is that as our tribal structures evolved and eventually became societal in nature (roughly 100,000 years ago), we moved away from an egalitarian way of life and became patriarchal and elitist. Instead of seeing each member of society as equal and as having an important role to play, we developed hierarchies and created poverty – displacing wealth and resources. The one thing, however, that we kept was the propensity to punish anyone who went against the grain of the status quo. Whether or not our personal interests were at stake by this other's person's actions, we still sought to punish them because punishing them meant bringing the wayward member of society back into a governable position that promoted the survival of the tribe's genetic code.

We had also begun seeking out stronger genetic influence by mixing with other groups and this is what we owe the terrible teens to. [2] Yes, your teenager isn't just filled with the seething rage of hell for you because they're going through hormonal changes. They're reacting this way toward you, as their parents, because of evolution – because we stopped inbreeding many moons ago and saw that genetic blending led to far superior beings on all fronts. [3] This, in turn, has left a mental imprint on humankind that kicks into effect just as soon as we are physically ready and able to have children. For the conservative parents who don't want to hear this, you might want to skip over this next sentence and head to the next paragraph. These children – the ones who become teenagers and start thinking their parents are stupid – are ready to have children at that very moment. Yes, your teen (or tween) daughter would have been married off to a good, strong boy from a neighbouring tribe just as soon as her menstrual cycle showed up. Just about everything that we feel we know about having children and raising them stems from practices that are rooted in instinct – many of which we've chosen to stop practicing anyway.

So, you see, it's really no surprise that people feel incited by those who refuse to fall in line with the evolutionary chain of events. To halt a bloodline is to ensure that the tribe cannot survive. You're basically killing your parents' bloodline by putting an end to the baby-making initiatives in your family. While a lot of what they might throw your way in their verbal barrage is connected to their own indoctrination and upbringing, there is an equal measure of primitive instinct at play.

The long and short of it: their rational, loving selves might want what's best for you, but their instinctive selves want what's best for the tribe and you having children is genetically what's best for the tribe. So, the next time you feel some type of way about your family members poking the bear that is your personal life, think about those poor Neanderthals that wanted nothing more than to survive.

And, no, please do not refer to your Aunt Janet* as a modern-day Neanderthal at your next family gathering.

Signs in the Animal Kingdom

I want to linger on an argument that I can see cropping up as a result of something that I touched on in the last section – females staying back at the cave, kraal, or hut to care for the young of the tribe while men went out to hunt. There will be a handful of men (and women alike) who crack wise and insist that if we're nothing more than cavepeople cum nomads who settled down and got all cleaned up, then why don't we follow those norms? Why don't we stay home, make babies, and care for them?

The answer is simple, but I'll take the long road home just so that we can finally get this point solidified. If we look at the animal kingdom, there are countless signs that our animal instincts weren't the only ones worth pursuing. They were just the ones that worked for our particular species. Lionesses hunt as opposed to lions. Male seahorses give birth as opposed to female seahorses. Male peacocks have prettier plumage. Male penguins protect their eggs until they hatch. The list goes on and on.

The key amongst all of these species and every other specie on the face of the earth is that they adapted to the environment and made survival choices – which became instincts – based on the prevailing conditions. To put it plainly, they altered their behaviour to suit their surroundings. If you can't see how this is exactly what women people are doing today by making the choice to be childless, then I'm not sure of how else to explain it to you. We are meant to adapt to the world around us or we end up dying out.

Now, here comes the next argument that I can foresee. People are going to say that I'm failing to see how refusing to have children is literally going to lead to the human race dying out, but I beg to differ. The population has consistently grown year on year despite the fact that women have chosen to put off their childbearing years and, in some cases, avoid them altogether. People are still having children – just not the people who really don't want to.

Besides, what kind of life would you want a child to have? Do you think children should be born to parents who don't want them? Do you think children should be born into unnecessary emotional and mental suffering? Do you think a child should have to bear the brunt of someone's unresolved trauma simply because their parents fell into the peer pressure of having children by a certain age?

Before you think that this is my way of posturing or squaring up for a heated debate on pro-life vs. pro-choice, it isn't. That, perhaps, is a book for a different day and I don't find that either personal belief system has space in this book nor should they be considered at this stage simply because we're discussing whether or not to have children.

With that little disclaimer out of the way, let's circle back. If you feel like a child should have to suffer due to any of those issues just so that we can keep populating the earth, you clearly have a heightened sense of self-importance. It shouldn't have to matter what beliefs, creeds, cultures, or religions you subscribe to for you to see how we need to work on our own moral, environmental, and social dilemmas before we bring another set of human beings crashing into this era of existence.

The third and final argument is that I, myself, am cherry-picking from the historical data by agreeing with historical human adaptability and not historical procreation habits. I don't see this as cherry-picking because adaptability is the only trait that should be unequivocally true for every single member of a species to survive. We adapt or we die. Making babies, however, is just a means for genetic survival. There are many tribes in the animal kingdom that have "spinsters" in their midst. There are childless animals just as there are childless humans and, still, those species seem to thrive.

So, I gave up the idea – quite some time ago, as I said – that the weight of the world should rest on my shoulders. I am not the incarnation of a Biblical Eve. I am not meant to repopulate the earth. I am more than my uterus and my ability to carry life. While it's an amazing biological function, the awe of which is not lost on me, it's not something I ever care to pressure myself into experiencing.

I'll fill you in on the many reasons why later on in this book but, for now, let's look at how normal this pressure is.

Through the Statistic Looking Glass

I feel a deep need to normalize the choice of being childless and destigmatize unrealistic expectations of women. If we take the statistical approach there is a lot to be uncovered on whether our approach to female fertility is normal or unrealistic. To lift the curtain on this polarity of thinking, let's look at the 140 million+ children who are born annually. By the time they reach a primary (or elementary) school age, 61 million of them will be kept home from school for lack of funds or other resources. A whopping 53% of those children will be girls and they might go off to join the 168 million child labourers. One of them might die every 17 seconds and all before they reach the age of 5. Those that do reach the age of 5 and manage to stay in school will walk to class with an empty belly and 69 million of them will suffer the effects of malnutrition. [4]

For those 140 million children that are born annually, there are already 153 million children who are in orphanages waiting for their happy ending. This isn't a soapbox speech or rant based purely on loosely gathered statistics. These are more than facts and figures on pieces of paper. They are little lives that might have been affected by the choices of people who thought they should have children just because they could or who didn't think at all.

Chapter 1

In the type of capitalist, elitist world that we live in today, having a child isn't as easy as laying down to make one. There is so much to consider. In the United States alone, families end up in unbelievable amounts of hospital debt just to bring a new life into the world. These aren't small amounts either; they're amounts to the tune of hundreds of thousands of dollars to bring one life into the world. For the families that do not have the financial means (or the health insurance) to cover this, they're bringing a child into the world and starting a new journey with heaps of debt already strapped to their backs.

In Africa, on the other hand, the cost of medical care might not be as expensive and there are public facilities that families can take advantage of. However, basic wages are far below livable amounts and public medical facilities have their own set of issues that we won't get into here.

In Europe, medical care is free in most countries and for most procedures but, again, these facilities are not always reliable. Young mothers – especially women of colour – are often subjected to low levels of support in such facilities, which leads to higher infant mortality rates, birth complications, and traumatic birth experiences. We have become so accustomed to trauma around the world that it has become something that is almost expected of us. You hear sentiments like, "Pain is beauty," and "No pain, no gain" and there is this overarching theme that we are meant to suffer for the standards and norms that society has deemed for us. The fact that 45% of women report having a traumatic childbirth experience is proof of this fact. [5] These include instances of near-death experiences during childbirth as well as postnatal trauma, such as unexpected birth defects in their newborn child, adverse health effects that lead to prolonged hospitalization for both mothers and their newborns, and abuse or maladministration that is carried out by medical staff.

At the end of the day, the statistics are stacked against those who insist that having children is the most fulfilling and rewarding aspect of life. Perhaps this was once true before women had the option of doing literally anything else other than having children. Perhaps it was true during wartime when having a little life to fight for and survive for served as a source of wholesome motivation to persevere. However, in this day and age – where life is cripplingly more expensive and we have to be far more productive [6] than previous generations – we are faced with a confluence of social and environmental factors that have edged us towards a slightly more self-focused frame of mind.

And there is nothing wrong with that!

There is absolutely nothing wrong with wanting a better life for yourself primarily before you even begin to fathom bringing another life into this world. More importantly, you shouldn't have to justify the fact as if you're on trial before a jury of your friends, family, and peers. It's simply nobody else's business and there are just no two ways about it. If no one else is willing to foot the medical bills you might face, stay up with you at night as your mental health fades to nothing, or hold your hand through difficult decisions regarding your child's physical well-being, they don't get a say. If they don't pay any of your bills, they don't get a say. In fact, even if they do help you with a few of your bills, they still don't get a say.

Your life, your body, and your decisions are not for sale!

Only you have the right to make choices that are as permanent and life-altering as having children.

Chapter 1

*

Ultimately, pressuring women (as well as men) and couples alike into having children has become the norm. It is felt in unspoken side glances, questions, and overt statements to the effect that every man, woman, and couple would be better off with children. Not only has this unwritten rule of how we should live our lives seeped into the very fabric of our societies, but it has done so with such vigor that the expectations transcend every language and cultural barrier imaginable. No matter where you're from or what beliefs you subscribe to, you will reach the age of 30 (or younger in some regions of the world) and you will be asked:

"So, don't you think you should start thinking about kids?"

CHAPTER 2 – ANTIQUATED STEREOTYPES THAT PREVAIL

The stereotypes and perceptions surrounding childlessness can be harmful and they need to be addressed. For some odd reason, we have a penchant for trying to "figure out" why a person lives their lives the way that they do. Because we have decided to live one way, we feel the need to make sense of someone who lives another way. This pendulum, unfortunately, swings both ways. In as much as people with children seek answers for why other people don't have children, there are just as many childless people who cannot wrap their heads around the way that people with children live. Parents get side-eyed on planes, trains, and buses. They get looks of judgment and disdain when their children throw tantrums in stores, make noise in restaurants, or kick up a fuss at the beach.

If you ask me, we could all do with a little more understanding.

So, for the parents who have gone through all of that judgment and know just what that feels like, why would you want to do that to someone else? Why would you want the polar feeling of shame that you've felt once before to be projected towards a childless person?

I don't think you do.

Deep down, none of us want to feel that way or make someone else feel that way. We want to support and uplift one another, but we can't get past our own pain for long enough to realize that it is where our judgment of other people truly stems from. There is no right, or wrong, way to live. The sooner we realize that we're all just human beings who are entitled to experience their fleeting time on earth as they see fit, the sooner we'll all be set free.

What a simple and beautiful life we would all lead if we were set free from:

- Judgment.
- Stereotypes.
- Negativity.
- Misplaced anger.
- Controlling tendencies.

These are just to name a few, but I believe you get the gist of it. With that said, let's explore some of the more common stereotypes and myths surrounding childlessness.

Women are Meant to Stay at Home

This is a loaded statement and one that I'll gladly pick apart. The idea of women staying home to rear children being something that should apply across the board is ludicrous. Quite possibly the most obvious issue here is that single-income households cannot afford to cover child-related expenses as well as the living expenses of another adult. While there are those who can afford this lifestyle and, perhaps, aspire to it, the vast majority of couples are not in a position to live like this. Stereotypes such as these are shameful considering what century we're in and they put unnecessary pressure on couples to fall in line with that idealistic way of life. What's worse is that couples – some of which don't even really want to have children – will end up fighting over this issue. Some men might think that their partners should stay home with children but their partners have no desire to do so. This could lead to conflicting interests in the relationship and even a complete forgoing of having children. If both parties are unable to reach an amicable middle ground, it could either prevent them from having children or lead to the demise of their relationship. Either way, they're going to remain childless for a little while longer. Let's face it, this is not the equivalent of compromising on what to have for supper.

Then there are women who might feel as though their partners are unambitious and should be working harder so that they can have a baby, whom she can then stay home with. Yes, that's correct. It isn't always that women don't want to have children but that they have expectations[1] that are not being met. As such, she might not feel like she's in a secure enough position to have a child. And while you or I might think that this is nonsensical, who are we to judge what she expects or wants out of life?

The fact is whether one or both parties want one party to stay at home with a child or neither of them do, the global financial and economic climate is not entirely conducive to the lifestyle. The plain truth is that the roles, in many aspects, have been equalized or even reversed. There are women who earn just as much as their partners and many who out-earn their partners by a mile. Now, I have to be cautious about where I put my feet with that statement

---

[1] Expectations – Whether the expectations between two romantic partners are realistic or fair in nature or quite the opposite is irrelevant. One person will, more often than not, have expectations and this can be cause for them not to take the leap to have children.

because they may, very well, just end up in my mouth. Here's what I mean when I say that women earn more than their partners. For one thing, I'm not stating that women earn more in the same fields. If you have a heterosexual couple who are both accountants and have the same number of years of experience, the male party would most likely be earning more. So, I am not purporting that the gender pay gap is not still a real thing (because it is!) What I'm actually referring to is the fact that there are many couples whose technical skills and pay lean in favor of the female party.

In simpler terms, there are a lot more stay-at-home dads these days.

Is there anything wrong with this?

Again, who are we to judge?

However, being a stay-at-home parent is not all that it's cracked up to be. The workload is constant and the job is thankless. Moreover, the decision to stay home with children often comes into play when the cost of care per child outweighs what one of the parents earns. The stay-at-home parent, therefore, loses their autonomy for the sake of saving the family a bit of money. Then, by the time the children are of an age where they no longer require constant care, that parent has been out of the work market for so long that finding a job that is commensurate with their standard of living seems like an impossible and pointless pursuit.

Finally, some women just don't see staying home with a child for any period of time as something to be desired. They don't see relinquishing their autonomy and power to someone else as living la dolce vita. It's just not on many of our radars anymore.

Chapter 2

The Motherhood Penalty

Let's hypothesize, for a moment, that there is no issue with finances and that both partners will return to work after their baby is born. This is assuming that one party will be opting for paternity leave just as well as the mother in this scenario will be opting for maternity leave. Childcare isn't an issue and just as soon as their baby is ready to be amongst strangers, they're back off to work. If that's the case, kudos to them, but they're going to run into something they weren't prepared for along the way: the motherhood penalty and the fatherhood bonus.

For the father, life is looking rosy. He has had some time off to care for his newborn child and bond with both his wife and child. At work, there is this sense of accomplishment for being able to replicate his DNA in tiny human form and this is followed by longing "oohs" and "aahs" as he shares photos of his baby. This is much to the delight of his colleagues who don't miss the opportunity to tell him what a wonderful father and modern man he is. As a parent, he will seem more stable and dependable, and, believe it or not, he will be one of the first people whose name gets thrown in the "raise and promotion" pot when the time comes.

For the mother in this equation, things are never truly the same as they once were. Unless she comes off as cold and calculating, speaking about her children will make her seem weak and airheaded. She'll be asked whether she's considering leaving the office for good now that she has a child to care for and the other childless people in her midst will question how she can stomach leaving her precious baby alone with a stranger. She might also be the likeliest person on the chopping block when layoffs roll around as opposed to her husband – even if they work for the same company! Ultimately, each child will cost her in terms of earning potential while each child will work to her partner's benefit.

Let's recap (and add to) the ways in which a mother is penalized and a father is benefitted by having a child. [7]

Motherhood Penalties	Fatherhood Bonuses
• Career choices are questioned. • Possible non-renewal of contracts. • Reduced wage increases by comparison to male and non-parent counterparts.	• Career moves are admired. • Possible promotions on the horizon. • Increased wage increases by comparison to female and non-parent counterparts.

Table 2: Motherhood Penalties vs. Fatherhood Bonuses

The statistics show that non-married, childless women make up to 96% of what their male counterparts make. This is as close as the gender pay gap has ever been and this is not something any of us would care to give up with the state of inflation. However, it is, indeed, something that we give up when we have children because some studies suggest that for each child that a woman bears, she loses up to 6% of her earning potential. For some reason, the professional world just doesn't see us as valuable as we once were before having children. There is also the theory that, for the sake of equality, bosses look women with children over for promotions because they're afraid of it seeming like they're offering her a promotion (and subsequent raise) just because she has children. Finally, there is the fact that women still tend to take on most of the load where afternoon activities and ferrying children around are concerned.

If someone walked up to you and asked you to earn less, dampen your career prospects, risk your life, lose sleep for up to 6 years, and stress about the well-being of another person for the rest of your life, would you be Eager Enid or Hesitant Hannah?

I know which side of the fence I'm sitting on and why. Other than the fact that some partners cannot fill the gap that their wives' pay loss would leave, there is also the issue of partners who begin holding things over their wives' heads. I would not want to put myself in a position whereby the person I love and trust is bullying me, imposing unrealistic expectations on me, or is otherwise unable to cover my needs to the standard that I am accustomed to. And, no, that is absolutely not a form of victim-shaming. Nobody puts themselves in positions to be bullied or abused.

The Nurture Conundrum

Does my previous statement make me cold and nonnurturing? I don't think it does. In our bid to make women the center of the nurture files – and the reason why children are either whole or unstable – people have to put us into one of two categories. These categories are:

- Nurturing.
- Nonnurturing.

I have two primary wiles where this black-and-white thinking is concerned. One – there are many ways that we, as human beings, can exhibit our nurturing side that doesn't involve having children. Two – so what if we aren't nurturing? Is that really the end of the world?

Let's unpack both of these arguments, starting with the notion that we can be nurturing and exhibit this behavior in other ways. There are countless childless women who are loving and kind towards the very same children that are yelled at by their strung-out, stressed-out mothers. These are women who take the time to sit with their nieces, nephews, and friends' children just to ask them what they're feeling and going through. This isn't something that is applicable to all childless women in the same way that being nurturing is not applicable to every woman who has produced a child. Being nurturing and being able to procreate are not synonymous with one another. In the animal kingdom, there are dozens of mothers who leave their offspring to fend for themselves, who abandon their young, and who even eat their own young! Yes, we are different animals altogether, but the point is that being childless is not a sign of being cold and unloving in the same way that having a child is not a sign of being a good, loving mother. I could sooner be more loving and nurturing to a puppy than some women are to their own children, so we need to stop correlating motherhood with warmth and love and everything else with tyranny and menacing comportment.

The second argument was whether being nonnurturing is really the end of the world. Women aren't supposed to be anything other than what they want to be. They do not need to fit into the box of what society deems acceptable of their behaviour. If a woman wants to step into more of her masculine energy than her feminine energy, so be it. This brings us straight back to the principle of living and letting others live. There are so many times when we turn a blind eye and allow others to just get on with their lives and, yet, when it comes to the baby conversation, we're all in. The gloves come off and all of a sudden everyone and their aunty is an expert on declining populations and women's health.

Yet, what we're really harping on about when we state, categorically, that women who do not bear children are strange and unusual is that we find it unnatural. It is our desire to cling to what we've been preprogrammed into believing is "natural" for women that keeps us stuck in this rut of wanting women to have children. Again, this is based on instinct, not rational thinking. Because our primitive minds know that typical females (any living being with a uterus) are supposed to produce little replicas of themselves, any female who cannot, will not, or doesn't want to have children is seen as unnatural. Now, because these particular females seem unnatural, they also come off as a threat – and this is for two reasons.

The first is that there is a threat to the longevity of the tribe's survival. If you didn't already know this, whether people like you or not, your proximity to them subconsciously places you on the fringes of their "tribe". To a certain degree, because of that proximity, you actually are. So, whether these are people that you work with, close friends, neighbours who you often converse with, or actual family members, you are a part of them and they are a part of you. The degrees of connection may vary, but even they won't be able to recognize exactly where the trigger stems from when they grimace and blurt out, "Why wouldn't you want to have children?"

The second is that, to the primitive human, anything that was unknown was seen as a threat. That mental state has persisted over the millennia and any woman who was seen as different from the lot was vilified. The Salem Witch Trials of 1692 are some of the more prominent examples of this. Due to the fact that most people cannot fathom not wanting children or not following the status quo that puts this expectation on them, the woman who doesn't want children is seen as alien or threatening. However, because it's morally unconscionable (and prosecutable) to burn a woman at the stake for being different, we just verbally assault them instead.

Imagine that.

Barren or Unbearable

This has to be one of the more laughable stereotypes out there and it's that women who say they don't want to have children are either barren or are unbearable to be around. In other words, there is no man on planet Earth that would want to have a baby with these women because they are absolute dragons. Nothing could be further from the truth and, here's a newsflash for you, not all women feel validated by the number of men that want to have a baby with them. It's just not that important to some of us.

But, while we're on this subject, let's discuss it a little further. Roughly 17% of the global population will struggle with infertility. That is 1 in 6 people. [8] Let's look at it this way. If you held someone's hand in preschool, or kindergarten, and had your first kiss in high school; maybe fooled around with a couple of people in college, one of them would have had infertility issues at some point in their adult years. That means that you or someone you know, but most likely a few people that you know and could have wound up with, are infertile. The emotional drain that wanting children, and not being able to have them, puts on these people is incredibly taxing. But we'll look at this in broader detail later on. I don't want to get ahead of myself, but I wanted to point out that the stereotype of being infertile is hurtful to both those who are and those who aren't.

In the event that you aren't having fertility difficulties and you go the unnecessary extra mile of telling someone that you aren't, they might consider you an unbearable person who cannot find a suitable mate because of that same insufferable attitude. While studies are conflicted on whether women are truly happy when they're childless (and in some cases unmarried), there seems to be regional tipping of the scales. In some parts of the world, women who are childless consistently prove to be the happiest group of people. However, in other regions, the majority of childless women appear to have the shortest and most uneventful lives in comparison to their child-bearing counterparts. And before you start a tirade on how this is evidence that women are better off having children, I'd like to point you in the direction of my book's subtitle, with particular reference to the "P.S. Motherhood is Not for Everyone" part. Being childless is not for everyone and motherhood is not for everyone. What we do know is that the metrics lean in favour of the nations where healthcare, childcare, and lifestyle are secure and the general pace of life is moderate. In regions where productivity is seen as some gilded trophy to be attained at all costs, women without children are happier. However, that isn't the consensus for all women in these countries. Where I live, for example, childcare is incredible. In fact, the World Economic Forum has consistently noted Sweden as being the best in the world where childcare is concerned. In the case of family living standards, Sweden is only second to the Netherlands. [9] In theory, we should all be wanting to have children, right? Well, we don't live in a world of hypotheses and theories. Even if countries such as this, a woman still has every right to say that she doesn't have a desire to birth or raise children.

We're happy women. We live in happy countries. Some of us have happy partners. Just because we do not want to have children, that does not mean that we are unbearable to be around. This is just one of those stereotypes that help others process something that is unnatural or unusual in their eyes. A woman's sexual orientation, religious beliefs, fertility status, temperament, and attitude have nothing to do with whether or not she wants to have a child. This is just something that we're all going to have to learn to accept.

Procreation for the Greater Good

Since we're discussing acceptance, we really should be looking at accepting that procreation is no longer for the greater good of humanity – especially not right now. At the risk of sounding unpatriotic, it is not my job to save any country's declining population. We are products of our environments and if our environments are not conducive to new human life, why should we continue bringing them into those environments – in the hopes that things will get better one day in the future? I think not.

The planet is gravely overpopulated. The statistics are staggering, proving that we are reaching such high numbers that we will not be able to share this planet with future generations of human beings, let alone other species. This fallacy that we – the childless – are causing depopulation is ludicrous. If you look at the reasons for declining populations in certain regions, you'll see that people prioritize taking care of the elderly because they have a healthy, long-living, aging population. There is not much room for newer generations because there are elder family members to take care of.

Just because one country's population is declining, that doesn't mean they all are. As I said before, it's not my (or any other woman's) responsibility to repopulate a nation. I could get into how we should all be seen as one race – the human race – and that we should be focusing on caring for all of those orphans and children living below the poverty line, but that's a conversation for another book perhaps. Nonetheless, there are far too many humans here anyway and one could argue that we are intuitively solving the problem as we have always evolved to do so. But that's just a theory and I do not like to live in hypotheses. If we look at the facts, we will see that countries that embrace the idea of importing their workforce solve many of the so-called problems that their declining population poses for them. America, for example, has one of the youngest populations [10] on the planet and it is because they have the highest number of immigrants [11] of any country in the world. They import their talent and youthful workforce (whether they all care to admit it or not).

It's worth considering that procreation, like many other aspects of life, is not an absolute good or evil. It's a complex issue with many factors to consider, such as environmental impact, societal norms, and individual choice. Some might argue that procreation can have a positive impact on society, such as the creation of new ideas, advances in technology, and the expansion of the workforce. However, others might argue that the negative impact of overpopulation and environmental degradation outweighs these benefits. Both arguments have their merits. Ask a researcher how they decide right from wrong with arguments of that nature and they'll tell you that, in most cases, there are no right and wrong answers – only the ones we can back up with research.

Despite these antiquated ideals, the decision to procreate should be a personal choice made with careful consideration of one's own values and beliefs, as well as the impact that choice may have on future generations and the planet as a whole. It's important to approach this decision with an open mind, recognizing that there is no one-size-fits-all answer and that different perspectives and beliefs should be respected. That is all we're looking for, after all: respect. This is something, along with common decency, that many people fail to practice. To live in a world where people can live their truth as freely as possible is the ultimate goal. Being able to share a space whether we choose to have children or not should be a given.

*

All one has to do is think of how many other hurtful stereotypes have since been deemed inappropriate to see that anything which harms another human being is not something that they should be partaking in. Yet, the majority of human beings insist on being on the wrong side of history while the lone wolves silently, and thanklessly, try to bring light to the issues that be. It's high time we put a stop to that if you ask me.

CHAPTER 3 – WHY WE'VE GONE CHILDLESS

T he societal norm of motherhood is one that has become increasingly toxic because the conversations around whether or not a woman should have a child are becoming ever more public. While matriarchs have almost always drilled their would-be predecessors about when they intend on taking the relay baton and carrying the torch of motherhood, there is an issue that we're not discussing. The issue is that we, as a society, have developed and women are doing so much more on different fronts than ever before. However, they're expected to do that and continue doing just as much on the home front as well. At the risk of sounding like the chauvinists who say, "You can't have it all, honey," it sure is shaping up to be a difficult task. That said, whether you can have it all depends on the support systems that you have in place as well as the mentality of the people around you.

For many women who are childless by decision, but not by choice, the decision to be childless was made because they could see right through the façade of their environment. They could see that they would be twice as tired; earn half as much and be expected to do triple the work in every aspect of their lives. Whether you feel like you've made the decision because you didn't have a choice or you made an active choice because you had multiple options is neither here nor there. The reasons 'why' shouldn't have to matter and, yet, for many of us they do.

For many of us, the questions are so constant and so bold that we start to question our own rationale.

Maybe they're right.

Maybe we're going to regret this one day.

Maybe one child wouldn't hurt.

These are the delusional conversations we start having with ourselves in our minds as we begin likening children to candies and thinking "Just one won't hurt." This must come to a swift end.

You should assure yourself that your maternal instincts are so on-point that you're willing to not have your potential future babies in a bid to protect them from the world. You are such a loving and nurturing person that you are willing to forego an experience because you don't want to add to the world's burgeoning problems and impact a little life in the process. You are a logical and wonderful human being who is willing to admit that children just aren't for you and that you wouldn't want to bring another life into the world for the sake of having children just because you're able to.

As you can see, there are so many reasons why women have decided to go childless, so let's take a deep dive into some of the more prominent reasons.

There are No Villages

There is no coming together and celebrating this new life and taking care of it as a tribe. The emergence of new life used to be an event – something that everyone would gather around to behold. Now, it's just congratulations; here are some clothes and a few gifts. People snap a few pictures, tell you that they're there if you need them, and then you're on your own. The village is all for show and offers little support to none. This is one of the many reasons why the choice to be childless is becoming more prevalent.

For centuries, the village concept has been an integral part of society, providing support and guidance to families as they raise their children. In this traditional model, a community of individuals comes together to offer their skills, knowledge, and resources to help each other thrive. However, in modern society, the village concept has largely disappeared, leaving families to navigate the challenges of parenthood on their own. Moreover, women are talking about it! A woman will tell her closest friends about her experiences in early motherhood. She'll complain that she didn't have enough support and that she felt lost or lonely. This means that childless women have a lot more knowledge about the process of motherhood than ever before. As it turns out, with this information on file, many of us don't want those experiences.

Go figure!

So, what has caused this rift in society? One of the key reasons for the loss of the village concept is the breakdown of traditional family structures. In the past, extended families often lived close to one another, providing a built-in support system for parents. Grandparents, aunts, uncles, and cousins would all pitch in to help raise children, providing a sense of continuity and stability for young people. However, in today's mobile society, families are often spread out across the country or even the world, making it difficult to rely on extended family members for support. Plus, people are also opening up about the rampant abuse that occurred in these systems as parents often left children home alone with family members whom they thought they could trust but actually couldn't. Stories of rape, molestation, and physical violence that took place in familial households are enough to turn anyone's stomach. This isn't just an unwarranted fear. It's an actual issue. Have a look at the stats on the matter.

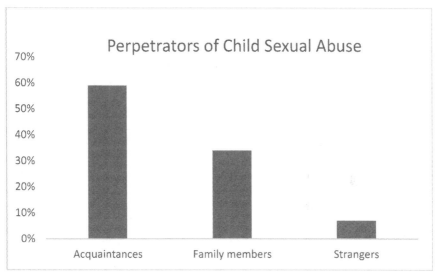

Figure 1: Child Sexual Abuse Statistics[2]

In some cases, people don't have a village due to work circumstances and in other cases, people just can't trust their village. The more we become aware of the social ills that creep into our family structures, the more the rise of individualism in modern culture prevails. In the past, people were more likely to view themselves as part of a larger community, with shared values, beliefs, and goals. However, in today's world, individual achievement and personal success are often prioritized over collective well-being. This shift in mindset has led to a decline in social capital, or the networks of relationships and trust that bind

---

[2] Courtesy of RAINN: https://www.rainn.org/statistics/children-and-teens

individuals together. Without strong social connections, parents are left to navigate the challenges of raising children largely on their own. For better or worse, many of us are now on our own. Without the support and guidance of a larger community, we may struggle to provide the resources and opportunities that children need to thrive.

In addition, children may miss out on the social and emotional benefits of growing up in a tight-knit community. Our primary agenda as the human race is to feel a sense of belonging and community. In traditional village cultures, children were often surrounded by a diverse group of adults, who provided role models, mentors, and sources of wisdom. The benchmarks upon which they built their own personalities, hopes, desires, and ambitions were deep and varied, leading to adults of equal depth. They learned to navigate the complexities of social relationships. Without these experiences, children may struggle to develop the social skills and emotional resilience they need to adapt to the fast-paced world they find themselves in.

Potential Recessions on the Horizon

The threat of an economic recession can have a significant impact on people's decisions about whether or not to have children. When economic conditions are uncertain, many individuals may be hesitant to take on the financial responsibilities that come with raising a family.

Why?

Well, if I don't know from one day to the next whether I'm going to have a job in the morning, adding a lifelong expense, such as a child, is less than ideal. All we're hearing about, at the moment, is the fact that artificial intelligence will only continue getting smarter and more adept at doing our jobs. Large multinational corporations (and small businesses) could start laying off people by thousands. Now is clearly not the time to be making any long-term financial commitments. This fear of job security is for the very fact that during a recession, businesses may be forced to downsize or close altogether, leading to higher unemployment rates and increased competition for available jobs. This can create a sense of instability and uncertainty, making it difficult for individuals to feel confident in their ability to support a family.

Even if you're lucky enough to keep your job, there's the possibility that the business you work for may cut back on employee compensation in order to reduce costs. This can make it more difficult for you to afford the high cost of living that comes with raising children, including housing, healthcare, and education. I'll say it again: it simply is not a good time to bring a child into the world. When economic conditions are uncertain, individuals may feel that it would be irresponsible or selfish to bring a child into an environment that may be characterized by financial stress and hardship. They may worry that they will not be able to provide the best possible life for their child, or that they will be unable to meet their child's basic needs. I've got to tell you that I tend to agree with them.

All of these factors can contribute to a decline in the birth rate during a recession. In fact, research has shown that birth rates tend to decline during periods of economic uncertainty and that they may take several years to recover once the economy stabilizes. So, it really should go without saying that we're not all chomping at the bit to have children and this is not something that should be probed by anyone for any reason. The problem isn't just that there aren't many supportive communities out in the world today, but also that having the right environment to raise a child in is becoming less available to would-be parents.

Some people, for example, were raised in an apartment. Their parents took them to parks and traveling was effortless because all they ever had to do was lock up and go. Life was simple and meaningful. However, those same people might not see it that way because of a phenomenon that often sees us growing up to want the very opposite of what our lives were as children. This is especially true if the copacetic nature of your life was only that way on the surface and there was turmoil behind closed doors. You might search for the reasons why your childhood wasn't as joyful as it should have been and, in so doing, conclude that everything your parents chose was unwittingly to your detriment. So, you decide that a house with a lawn and a white picket fence is the only environment that is suitable for a child – which it isn't – and you say that you will never bring a child into any other environment. If you cannot afford that house with a lawn and a white picket fence, and you choose not to have children because of the fact, that might simply be a choice you make because you personally believe it would not work out in a child's best interests.

Now, I will say this. There are millions of people around the world who live in various types of accommodation and successfully raise well-rounded, healthy children. Whether it is a childhood of strife in a certain environment that makes you shy away from it or the fact that you simply do not want to choose between sacrificing your career in the city or raising your child there, your choices are still valid.

Civil Uncertainty

The presence of civil riots and political uncertainty can have a profound impact on people's decisions about whether or not to have children. The fear of violence, instability, and uncertainty can create a sense of unease and anxiety that makes it difficult for individuals to feel confident in their ability to raise a family in a safe and stable environment. The thought of having to hide from or escape a turbulent situation that lies in wait for you just beyond your door is frightening enough as it is. The thought of having to do this with children in tow is another story altogether.

When civil riots and protests are taking place in a community, there is no way of knowing what might come next. Human beings are erratic and unpredictable at best. At our worst, we can be violent and completely devoid of respect for human life. As an already-overstimulate generation, we don't want to live through raising children through a civil war or the next world war. If I had children, I would want to be able to look them in the eye and assure them of their safety. I wouldn't want to recognize the depths of fear in their eyes as they recognize it in mine. While I don't want to make this book a political inquest, the political uncertainty that we are constantly subjected to is a fair reason why birth rates in certain regions are declining. We have men and women in suits who think that they have a right to play their own version of Battleship while our lives hang in the balance. More often than not, it isn't in a bid to ensure our freedom – it's all politically and financially motivated. With these unstable, war-inclined at the helm, we're all worried about the status and stability of our communities. Well, I say "all", but I really mean those of us who have the sense to be concerned with the current state of affairs. The possibility of conflict and instability, as well as the impact of political decisions, is far too heavy of a burden to carry.

Ultimately, the choices of others lead to us having to make our own choices to counter those decisions. These are decisions that have positioned us on the verge of a complete climate meltdown – yet another reason to stave off having children.

Climate Change

Climate change – an issue that has people divided and activists up in arms over the blatant disregard for what research shows us to be true. The truth is that no matter what we believe about climate change, it is impacting people all over the world, and it is having a significant impact on people's decisions about long-term commitments. From buying a home to having children, climate change is making individuals hesitant to make long-term commitments because they are unsure of what the future will hold.

As climate change continues to impact the planet, individuals are becoming more aware of the potential risks and challenges that lie ahead. They may worry about the impact of natural disasters on their homes and communities, or about the availability of resources such as food and water. We need only look back as far as the pandemic of 2020 to see how resources began drying up and grocery store shelves emptied out faster than we could say "vaccine". (Another subject of contention). This uncertainty can make it difficult for individuals to feel confident in their ability to make long-term commitments that will be sustainable and viable for the foreseeable future. There are those of us who don't feel comfortable committing to plans too long in advance because we just don't know how we will feel or what might be in store for us at that point. While this, arguably, has nothing to do with climate change, the point is that all of this uncertainty takes its toll on our desire to do anything that will have effects beyond next week Tuesday.

We're also one of the first generations to feel more responsibility towards future generations than towards our predecessors. As the impact of climate change becomes more apparent, individuals may worry about the legacy that they are leaving for future generations. They may feel a sense of responsibility to ensure that future generations are able to enjoy the same quality of life that they have experienced before they bring any more future generations into the equation.

Being childless by choice doesn't automatically make us cynics but there are pessimists amongst us. The sense of hopelessness about the future makes us question the point of trying to create a legacy. If any of you have begun feeling overwhelmed and discouraged by the scale of the problems that climate change presents, I don't blame you. Feeling like it's impossible to make a meaningful difference and that any long-term commitments that you make will be futile in the face of such a monumental challenge is understandable. We're faced with incredible challenges on the road ahead. The last thing we need to be worried about is expensive childcare or arguing with our partners over who is doing more work as a parent.

Expensive Childcare

Speaking of expensive childcare, the cost of childcare is a significant issue that is deterring people all over the world from having children. In many countries, the cost of childcare has skyrocketed in recent years, making it increasingly difficult for parents to afford the care that their children need. As a result, many couples are choosing to delay having children or forgo having them altogether. While the cost of childcare can vary significantly depending on the location and quality of care, in many places it is extremely expensive. This can be particularly challenging for families with lower incomes or for those who are just starting out in their careers. The trouble is that many people who are in the early years of their careers are also in the dying years of their fertility – especially in a woman's case. Nonetheless, the high cost of childcare can make it difficult for parents to afford the basic necessities of life and this makes having children unjustifiable in their opinions. If you think this isn't as bad as some make it out to be, have a look at the global figures before making your next statement.

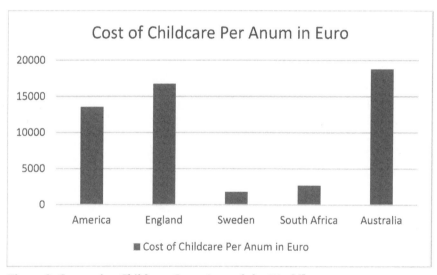

Figure 2: Comparing Childcare Costs Around the World[3]

---

[3] References: US Stat [12]. England Stat [13]. Sweden Stat [14]. South Africa Stat [15]. Australia Stat [16].

Imagine having to contend with hefty amounts to the tune of tens of thousands of euros per year and still be faced with a slow decline in your wage increases. Another reason why expensive childcare is deterring people from having children is the lack of support from employers and governments. In many countries, employers are not required to provide paid parental leave or other benefits that can help to offset the cost of childcare. Additionally, government support for childcare is often limited or non-existent, making it difficult for parents to access affordable care. This lack of support can make it difficult for parents to balance work and family responsibilities and can contribute to feelings of stress and burnout. In addition to the financial burden and lack of support, the quality of care is also a concern for many parents. In some countries, the cost of childcare is high, but the quality of care is low. This can be particularly concerning for parents who want to ensure that their children are receiving the best possible care and education. The lack of quality care options can make it difficult for parents to feel confident in their decision to have children.

The high cost of childcare is not just a problem for individual families; it also has significant economic and social implications. For example, when parents are unable to afford childcare, they may be forced to leave the workforce or reduce their hours, which can have a negative impact on their earnings and career prospects. Additionally, the lack of affordable childcare options can limit the ability of women to participate fully in the workforce, which can contribute to gender inequality and limit economic growth.

I'm sorry, but we've worked far too hard to get this close to complete earning equality in the workforce. We're not about to lose it all now.

Time-Consuming

We don't know if we're going to be alive tomorrow morning. What's the point of bringing a child into the world to suffer, die young, and eat into the little bit of joyous free time we have left? Yes, the argument of all of us being traumatized and living in a state of foreshortened future is a possibility. Perhaps we've been exposed to the negative effects of an unstable world for so long that we've finally snapped and sunken into a collective existential crisis. Maybe having children isn't the problem. Maybe there is something deeper that we're not looking into and I'll regret it one day. Either way, it's my life to regret! No one else has a right to chime in.

In recent years, couples all over the world are increasingly delaying or forgoing having children altogether. The lack of time that many couples feel they have to dedicate to raising children is one reason, but another is that many of us feel more inclined to focus our time on our own pursuits. Between the pressures of work, social obligations, and other responsibilities, we're left with little time for anything more. I will admit that there are probably more people wasting time and feeling like they have none than there are people who actually have no time, but it is still their prerogative whether or not to have children. Be aware that we spend a significant amount of time on our phones, computers, and social media feeds as well as responding to work emails. This constant distraction coupled with intense workloads and an inability to come down from a heightened state of physical and mental reactivity makes many people reluctant to consider the idea of having a child.

The lack of time for raising children can have significant implications for individuals, families, and society as a whole. For couples who do decide to have children, the lack of time can result in increased stress and burnout, which can negatively impact their relationship and the well-being of their children. This is not something that should ever be taken lightly. Countless people think that having a child will automatically solve their problems, but if you're already high-strung or otherwise unwell on the mental front, having a child will only worsen the problem. You will find yourself in a position where you barely know how to take care of yourself and, yet, you're responsible for taking care of another life. If, like many people around the world, you do not have a village like we looked at earlier, you're in for a world of hurt. There will be no downtime – especially in the first 4-6 years of your child's life. The parental workload will be constant and any void that you had hoped to fill will be so gaping and vacuous that you'll either face your problems head-on (which is great) or implode and suck everyone into the emotional black hole along with you.

I wouldn't recommend taking this type of risk to anyone.

If you value your downtime and you're the type of person that is already on mentally shaky ground, you need to stop and consider what adding a child into the equation would do to you. Don't put yourself in a position that will worsen any condition and do not think that a child will teach you patience or calmness. If you're a frazzled person who needs time to cool off and rationalize, you're not going to have that in the first couple of years. You will be overstimulated by constant physical contact with your children and the sounds that they emit as they learn to communicate in appropriate manners. If you handle that stage incorrectly, you're only going to be hurting your children in the long run. Subsequently, your lack of time for them will end up hurting you too.

For those who say time is a cruel mistress and that childless people will regret not having children when they're alone in an old-age facility or alone in their homes, here's yet another newsflash for you. It will be a lot more heartbreaking to sit and recount the reasons why your children never visit you than it will be to sit and recount all the memories of a life well-lived with maybe – I'll give it to you – a tiny hint of questioning what could have been with regard to a child.

Children do not fill a void. They do not give you more time.

They make you painfully aware of your shortcomings and take up every shred of free time you will ever have.

*

When all is said and done, there are many more reasons – some of which are automatic or unconscious – why people do not have children. Changing the narrative on whether people, especially women, should have children is a must. There is already far too much stress in our world. The last thing any of us need is to be dealing with hurtful questions, side glances, or overtly rude comments about our personal choices. We can suffer fools and understand harmless interactions that aren't pressed. However, when the matter is constantly being pushed with little regard for how frustrating it must be for the person on the receiving end, there is clearly something wrong with the programming on the emitting end.

CHAPTER 4 – THE ELEMENTS OF THE DECISION-MAKING PROCESS

Now that you understand a bit more about the reasons why we've gone childless, I want to bring you into the decision-making process. Remember that there are going to be moments when I address those of you who are childless by choice and those of you who want to understand the choices of childless people. So, whether you're the former or latter individual, we're going to be exploring the elements that go into the decision-making process of whether or not to have children.

First of all, I should clear something up. For some people, it isn't such a calculated decision as I'm about to depict. In the same manner that it's second nature for some people to have children, it's second nature for others to not have children. They don't go down the rabbit hole of why they don't want to have children. They simply embrace the fact, honour how they feel about the situation, and get on with their lives.

Not everything in life requires deep introspection. Not every decision we make is the result of some mental issue that we need to deal with or unresolved childhood trauma. Sometimes, a decision based on intuition is just that and nothing more.

With that said, the elements that we're going to look at in this particular chapter will explain a handful of the more prominent areas that people assess when they're deciding whether or not to have children.

Looking at Your Relationship

This is a big one. If you're in a committed relationship, partnership, or marriage, it's only normal to look at each other and ask, "Should we have kids?" It is completely possible for two people who once had no interest in having children to change their minds. It's also possible for them to question whether everyone else who has children is "on to something" by having them. It is also common for one party to start feeling broody while the other remains adamant that they do not want to have children.

Assessing whether or not your relationship is conducive to having children is important. If one of you is, indeed, considering the possibility while the other isn't, is this possibly a passing phase? Is there something that has triggered it? Maybe your best friend just bought a house and is expecting their first child with their spouse and it's giving you a case of FOMO. Whatever the case may be, you're on dangerous ground. In cases like this, if the relationship is not healthy or is codependent in nature, one party might give up their desires or compromise on what they want to keep their partner happy. More often than not, the partner who is adamant that they don't want to have children is the one who will give in to the desires of the partner who now wants to have a child.

It is to avoid this scenario that many couples choose to stick to their guns on their initial decision not to have children. Moreover, one party might not feel that they are in a relationship that would weather having children well. Does that mean that they think their partner is irresponsible? No. Does it mean that their partner is any less worthy of love? No. Does the party who feels that way know that they would rather be with their partner than throw their relationship away for the possibility of maybe being slightly happier with a living dependent in the situation? Yes!

One of the most significant factors that can make a relationship unsuitable for having children is financial instability. Raising a child can be incredibly expensive, from the costs of childcare and education to basic necessities such as food, clothing, and housing. If a couple is struggling to make ends meet or has significant debt, it may not be wise to add the additional financial burden of a child to their lives. Even if you are both financially sound, the possibility of buckling under the financial pressure of raising a child is likely. After all, it is usually financial concerns or invasive in-laws that lead to the demise of a relationship. If, for instance, you happen to have a child who requires extra medical attention after birth or has some form of chronic illness that makes it difficult for a child to adjust to society, the fights are bound to roll in. Before you know it, you'll be arguing over what brand of cheese to buy and pinching pennies to ensure that your child's life is as comfortable as it can be while you and your relationship suffer. It's not just the stuff of fiction. These are real issues that happen to real people all of the time.

Another factor that can make a relationship unsuitable for having children is emotional instability. Effective communication, healthy conflict resolution, and emotional regulation skills are essential for creating a stable and supportive home environment for children. If a couple is struggling with emotional issues such as depression, anxiety, or addiction, they may not have the emotional capacity to provide the kind of stable, loving home environment that children need to thrive. However, even if you have all of that checked out, having a child in today's world puts parents under unimaginable duress and all of those healthy coping mechanisms and communication styles can go right out the window after a period of prolonged stress.

Compatibility is another critical factor in determining whether a relationship is suitable for having children. Couples who have fundamentally different values, lifestyles, or life goals may find it challenging to create a cohesive and supportive family unit. What works for couples with vast differences when they're alone as a unit of two will not necessarily work when they add children to their lives. For example, if one partner values independence and travel while the other prioritizes stability and routine, they may struggle to find common ground in raising a child.

Looking at Your Current Schedule

If your schedule is crazy now, it's only going to get worse with children around. Either you or your children are going to have to compromise and it is most likely going to be you who ends up compromising. If you can't see yourself slowing down or removing anything from your schedule, then it's clear that now is not the time for you to have children. If you're nearing the end of your fertility window and this doesn't perturb you, it's safe to say that you are quite happy with being childless by choice.

The fact is that nothing is permanent – not even your current schedule, but having children is an undeniably permanent decision. What's more, you have to consider them in everything that you do. And please do not try to correlate having a pet (or several) with having children, because you cannot leave a child home alone all day and make up for it by taking them for a walk when you get back from work. Also, note that your expenses remain fairly stable throughout a pet's lifespan while your expenses only ever increase with a human being until they are between the ages of 18 and 28. Yes, despite your legal obligation to support your child coming to an end on their 18th birthday, you're not just going to throw them to the wolves. Studies already show that more and more adult children are choosing to remain in their parental homes and, in some cases, they still require financial aid to some degree well into their 20s. [17] Trust me, this is not because they want to. They'd rather be living on their own terms, but it's not always financially viable nowadays.

Consider your schedule interrupted for the next 25+ years!

In today's fast-paced world, many individuals are leading hectic lives, juggling multiple responsibilities and commitments both in their personal and professional lives. As a result, some may find the idea of having children daunting, if not outright impossible, given their current circumstances. Here are some reasons why a hectic schedule can prevent people from wanting to have children.

First and foremost, a busy professional life can make it difficult for individuals to devote the necessary time and energy required to raise a child. With long work hours, demanding deadlines, and heavy workloads, many people find themselves with little time or energy left over for their personal lives. This can make it challenging to develop and maintain a strong connection with a partner, let alone find the time and resources to devote to raising a child. In essence, if you don't have the time to take care of yourself, you might not have the time to take care of anyone else.

While many people in high-pressure professions have the financial stability necessary to raise a child comfortably and they can likely cover the costs of childcare, healthcare, education, and other necessities, they don't want to just leave their children with a nanny. For many of them who might have grown up that way, they know how lonely it was – particularly if they were an only child. There will always be a tradeoff in the decision-making process of whether or not to have a child and some people just aren't in a trading mood.

Whether or not you earn more than enough to have as many children as your heart desires, the pressures of maintaining a busy work schedule can often leave you feeling stressed, anxious, or overwhelmed. Many people may find that their careers require them to travel frequently, work long hours, or be on call 24/7. If one partner decides to take up the job of being a full-time parent while the other covers the bills (and can do this comfortably), then Bob's your uncle. If not, you're in for a wild and bumpy ride. If you already have a demanding schedule and you don't have a partner, or are having difficulty finding one, where do you even begin making a child?

We can chalk that one up as a point for being childless but not so much by choice.

Looking at Your Career Trajectory

In modern society, the expectation that women should prioritize having children over pursuing their careers is becoming increasingly outdated, but people are clinging to this antiquated lifestyle like their own lives depend on it. The idea that every individual should have the right to prioritize their career trajectory over having children, and the idea of women with goals, is practically blasphemy to some people. But demonizing women needs to come to an end – like yesterday.

Firstly, it is essential to acknowledge that everyone has their own values and goals. For some, the pursuit of a successful career may be a top priority, and that is perfectly acceptable. Women should not feel pressured to have children simply because it is expected of them by society. For some women, pursuing a career may be a better use of their time and resources, and they should be able to make that choice without judgment or criticism. Most women are going to do what they want anyway, so ramming beliefs down their throats about rearing children is just going to push them away. If you've done this to another woman, stop. If you're the woman to who this was done, keep on focusing on that career and staying in your lane. Others will get the picture soon enough.

Societal expectations placed on women are often rooted in patriarchal and misogynistic beliefs. These beliefs perpetuate the notion that women are inferior to men and should prioritize domestic duties over their professional aspirations. However, this mindset is not only harmful to women but also to society as a whole. When women are discouraged from pursuing their goals and aspirations, society misses out on the valuable contributions they can make in the workplace and beyond. If women stayed home to tend to children and aspired to do nothing more, we wouldn't have Marie Curie to thank for radioactivity theory or Maria Telkes for the first fully solar-powered house. We might have taken a little longer to develop computers and we might not have such advanced computers yet.

The concept of motherhood being the ultimate fulfillment for women is not only harmful but also untrue. Women can find fulfillment in various aspects of their lives, and their careers can be just as rewarding as motherhood. Who we raise is not as important as who we become because if we don't become any better, raising someone else is just going to have us creating more versions of ourselves. Women can contribute to society in many other ways and we are becoming game-changers and path-makers in a number of industries.

Additionally, prioritizing a career over having children can have significant benefits for women. Pursuing a successful career can provide financial stability, independence, and personal fulfillment. That autonomy can greatly reduce the number of women who stay in abusive relationships for fear of not being able to provide for their children. Furthermore, it is important to acknowledge that career success can also benefit future generations, as it can lead to more significant opportunities and advancements for women in the workforce. Remember, there are many children out there and we don't necessarily need to be worrying about populating the earth with future generations just yet. We're good on the population front!

Despite the benefits being clear and apparent, we're still labeled as selfish, obscenely career-focused, or even less feminine. It's incredible and quite funny to me how I could ever be labeled less feminine for not having children. These are all just gender stereotypes. Women should be free to make their own choices without fear of judgment or criticism. Besides, new mothers often complain about not being able to maintain their self-care regimens or step into their femininity for quite some time after the birth of each child. I witnessed my own sisters barely being able to keep up with life. Not to sound judgmental, but this doesn't sound like the epitome of femininity. So, to me, this is a bit of the pot calling the kettle black. If we could all just stop being so judgmental of one another and supported each other's choices, we would be so much better off than we are right now. Judgment leads to anger and anger leads to closeted resentment, which leads to overt aggression at some point. None of this is worth it.

Furthermore, it is essential to acknowledge that men do not face the same societal expectations when it comes to having children and pursuing their careers. Men are often encouraged to focus on their careers and are not expected to prioritize having children in the same way that women are. This double standard is unfair and reinforces gender stereotypes that have no place in modern society. Both men and women suffer because of these gender stereotypes. Who says men don't want to prioritize children? Who says they want to be pushed into working relentlessly? Who says they want their masculinity to be questioned just because they're not earning what society deems they should by a certain age?

It's all so toxic.

It is also important to note that having children is not the only way to build a family. Many women choose to build families through other means, such as adoption, fostering, or by choosing to co-parent with a partner or friend. These alternative family structures can be just as rewarding as traditional families, and they provide an opportunity for women to prioritize their careers first while still being able to build a family later if they want to.

Chapter 4
Looking at Your Financial Stability

I touched on this already, but it's important for us to dig a little deeper. There are two primary contexts in which this needs to be considered. The first is in the context of a couple and the second is in the context of a single woman. Now, before you tell me that you need a man to have a child, let's not forget what the recent decades of artificial insemination, surrogacy, and sperm donors have brought us. It is entirely possible for a financially independent woman to have and raise a child on her own, should she so choose. Whether not having a father figure or definitive masculine energy along with feminine energy is healthy for the child is of little relevance to the book at this juncture. Our focus is the fact that finances are often one of the larger deterrents where having children are concerned – whether the person considering it is in a relationship or not.

If you haven't got the finances for certain things, you aren't going to be able to afford a child. This is the plain and simple reality for many people in emerging generations. As the saying goes, many people are just one missed paycheck away from being homeless. If there are certain boxes that you cannot tick, then you would be wise to not consider yourself financially stable enough to have a child. These include:

Having little debt or none at all.	☐
Having an above-average credit score.	☐
Having a livable budget and being able to stick to it.	☐
Having an emergency fund equal to 3-6 months of expenses.	☐

Table 3: Financial Stability In a Nutshell

Having children is a big decision that comes with many responsibilities, especially financial ones. The expenses associated with birthing and raising children can add up quickly, and it's important for prospective parents to be aware of these costs when making the decision to have children.

Firstly, the cost of giving birth can be significant. Recent reports indicate that the average cost of a routine vaginal delivery in the United States is $14,768, while a cesarean can cost an average of $26,280. [18] You may also need to save for university or college tuition. Even if you live in a country that has free public colleges, what's to say that your child will want to attend such an institution? What if they don't offer the specialized field of study that your child wants to pursue? In the United States, the average 4-year degree will cost between $15,000 and $45,000. [19] Private colleges and universities will be far more expensive than this. In most European countries, we're covered by national healthcare systems that do not require payment for treatment, including prenatal care and delivery. Just like public hospitals, public schools are also free and, in some countries such as Denmark, the government pays you to go to university! [20] That being said, there are still costs such as afternoon activities, private lessons, specialist doctors, and more that we have to contend with and those do not come cheap.

Look, if we're all being honest with one another, we know that there are many people who don't tick all of the aforementioned boxes and who are still able to raise children. They don't just spontaneously combust because of the fact that they're not 100% financially stable when they have children. They survive. Many of them thrive. In fact, it's estimated that only 24% of young adults in developed nations are financially independent [21] while they only reach full financial stability by the age of 40. So, yes, it's possible to have children without being completely financially stable when they're born, but if you want to ensure that you're not scarring yourself or your children, something else needs to check out.

That's your mental health.

Looking at Your Mental Health

Postnatal depression is real! Let's start there and build on this. If you or anyone in your family has a history of mental health disorders, you need to consider how this might manifest for you. Healing from trauma and keeping a mental health issue in check can be done when you're in a stable routine and you're getting consistent sleep. However, when you're covered in breast milk, sweaty, clammy, feeling touched-out, and running on 2 hours of sleep – all while having to be alert and make sure your infant doesn't die – you might just go over the edge. As a matter of fact, that's enough to send anyone over the edge!

Postnatal depression (PND), also known as postpartum depression (PPD), is a mental health condition that affects quite a few women after they have given birth. It is estimated that around 1 in 7 women experience postnatal depression [22], which is a scary prospect if you think about the fact that severe cases can be fatal for both mother and child. Symptoms may include feelings of sadness, anxiety, exhaustion, difficulty bonding with the baby, changes in appetite and sleep patterns, and feelings of guilt or worthlessness. Many women have described the sensation of moderate to severe PPD as a feeling of inescapable sorrow. Their brain feels foreign to them and they begin to lose a grip on reality.

Quite possibly the worst part of it all is that PPD can occur at any time during the first year after giving birth, and may be caused by a combination of physical, emotional, and social factors. These can include hormonal changes, lack of sleep, difficulty breastfeeding, stress related to caring for a new baby, and – drumroll please – the pressure placed on women by society, family, and their partners![4]

PPD can be a challenging experience, but it's important to remember that it is a treatable condition and that with the right support and care, recovery is possible.[5] I don't want to make child-rearing seem all gloom and doom in case you are considering it and picked this book up to determine whether or not you should have a child. With anything in life, you have to trust your gut instinct. If you have doubts, it's often a sign that now is not the right time anyway.

Just bear in mind that every little piece of self-doubt that you have felt about yourself and your capabilities might be magnified after childbirth. If you're already a self-conscious person, you might send yourself in a tailspin as you second-guess every decision you make regarding your child and their well-being. This won't be a healthy way for you, or anyone in close proximity to you, to live. You'll be so wired from all of the calculations, recalculations, mom guilt, fear, and potential self-loathing that you'll, eventually, become your own mental undoing.

---

[4] NOTE: Treatment options may include counseling, medication, and support groups. In other words, more expenses that you might not be prepared for. It's also important to practice self-care.

[5] **DISCLAIMER: If you or someone you know is experiencing postnatal depression, don't hesitate to seek help from a healthcare professional.**

I know. This got incredibly dark exceedingly quickly, but I'm not here to sugarcoat this for anyone. I feel as though I've been tasked with setting the record straight and for that record to be straight, I need to be as candid about all of this as possible. Having very little time to focus on yourself and your mental health (or even just basic self-care) as a parent can worsen any mental condition and amplify it tenfold.

Looking at Your Free Time

As mentioned in the previous subsection, not having the time to focus on yourself, practice self-care, or take care of your mental health is not going to go down well. This is true whether or not you have any preexisting mental health conditions. Despite the fact that we looked at your schedule, which might include work as well as rituals and routines, we haven't stopped to talk about the joy of having free time.

There are times when being able to just exist without expectations is called for. In fact, it is needed for us to be able to reset our minds and function like normal human beings for the remainder of the week. Not being able to bathe, use the bathroom, go out and get your hair cut, or just nip to the grocery store very quickly to get something that you forgot without having to consider the hassle involved is not for everyone. Choosing between having lasagne without the bechamel sauce you forgot to buy or having to get the pram out from the hallway closet again and getting your baby into a thousand layers of clothes while they squirm around in protest before heading out into the cold isn't ideal for most people. I'm being facetious regarding the layers, of course.

Chapter 4

The fact is there will always be demands on your time. Saying goodbye to silent bubble baths, lying in darkness and enjoying the stillness of the night, or the ability to be spontaneous because you have some "free time" to do something would rattle some of the most selfless people. And being selfish, while we're on the subject, isn't an innately bad thing. It is arguably bad when it's practiced at the expense of the rights, deserved comfort, or well-being of others. However, taking care of yourself and prioritizing yourself without harming anyone in the process should be the standard.

With children around, your free time is always consumed by something – even if that "something" is just thinking of them and what is best for them. As it stands, childless adults are faced with making 35,000 decisions every single day of their lives. If they decide to have children, the number of mundane decisions increases dramatically as they are now accountable for another life. But the number of difficult decisions also increases dramatically, with an average of 1,750 [23] potentially life-altering decisions being made in the first year of a child's life alone.

The long and short of it: not even your mind will be "free" to do anything from the moment you commit to having a child.

*

As we progress, I want to reiterate that just because you agree with sentiments in this book, that doesn't mean you always will – and that's ok. I'm not trying to coerce or convince anyone of what they should or shouldn't be doing with their lives. All I am offering is an insight into being childless by choice, so that (hopefully) we can change the idea that this is the norm for everyone and put an end to hurtful commentary. These are just some of the elements that go into the decision-making process but, for some of us, we didn't expect there to be more benefits than we could count...but there were!

Chapter 5

CHAPTER 5 – THE BENEFITS THAT NO ONE TALKS ABOUT

This is where we shift our focus away from looking at why people make the decision to not have children. We'll still come back to this narrative every once in a while, but we're going to start focusing more and more on life without children. This is your midway point in this book and the beginning of the "childless by choice" positives. It would appear that people are more concerned with telling women why they should have children than they are with discussing the benefits of not having children. It's almost as if saying "not having children is great" is some type of taboo that makes people think that you'll want to eat their children. The look of sheer horror that women (who openly express their lack of desire to have children) get is honestly the most bizarre thing I've ever seen. I often find myself wondering why someone else's uterus is of such importance to other people, then I remember everything we've already looked at in earlier chapters.

Since the same people who insist on you having children won't discuss all of the benefits of not having children, I'll do it for them – starting with silence. Overstimulation is a serious issue for parents, particularly mothers. It is even worse for stay-at-home mothers because their children seek them out for everything. If children fall, they look for their mamas. If children are frightened, they look for their mamas. If children are hungry, cranky, sleepy, lonely, dysregulated, too hot, too cold, or otherwise inconvenienced they – say it with me – look for their mamas!

Having the silence, space, and freedom to not be constantly called upon, cried on, drooled on, hit, bit, or touched is something that I hold sacred. I don't detest children in any way. I would just rather not have that life of constant overstimulation. Just in case you were wondering, overstimulation has the ability to give you a sense of mental and physical discomfort.

That's not for everyone. I'm willing to bet that if we actually told would-be mothers what they were getting into, they would think it isn't for them either! (There's a phenomenon that makes mothers forget the severity of birth and sleep deprivations, just FYI.)

I digress!

Let's get into some of the amazing benefits of being childless by choice.

Time to Unwind

I'm going to give you two scenarios and you can decide which of the two sound better to you.

Scenario 1: You get home from a long day at the office, set your keys down on the kitchen counter, and open the fridge. You pull out a few ingredients and grab your phone before navigating to the Spotify app and putting on your favourite playlist. You pour yourself a glass of wine (or water – whatever floats your boat) and set to work on making yourself a hearty meal. When it's ready, you grab your plate, plop yourself down on the couch and watch your go-to pick-me-up show before hopping into an uninterrupted shower and getting a good night's sleep.

Scenario 2: You get home from a tiring day at work and trip over the very same bicycle that you keep telling your son not to leave in the front hall. You're instantly met with the sound of the TV, which is on a channel you keep telling them not to watch and it's turned up way higher than it should be. You're hungry, so you decide to pick your battles and head to the kitchen to get dinner going. Alas, there's a load of dishes in the sink because no one has bothered to wash them and, if you're going to cook, you're going to have to do it. Usually, you'd wrangle everyone and tell them how that's not your job, but with the day you've had, you would rather not argue. After cleaning up and cooking, you call everyone over to come and eat only for your child to say, "Chicken parm – yuck!" This is quickly followed by the fact that they have a school project due tomorrow that they haven't even started. You just want to go to bed, but you can't and, by the time everyone else is asleep, you're too tired to take that long, relaxing bath you've been dreaming about since lunch. You get into your pajamas and black out.

Which of these sounds better to you?

I'll wait while you ponder the answer.

For those who are going to say that nights aren't always like this, you make a valid point. However, for others, there aren't enough cute moments of cooing and "I love you, Mommy" to erase the nights like *Scenario 2*.

The truth is that, whether or not you have children, some nights are going to look more like you sitting in sweatpants and ordering something from your favourite fast-food joint. That isn't the point. The point is that you will have the freedom to choose exactly when that happens without feeling like you're a bad parent for serving your kids takeout for the third time this week. What's more important to many childless people is the fact that we can unwind when we're already going through a tough day. We're not going to come home to overstimulation or ungrateful behaviour that will worsen how we're feeling. It's no wonder there are so many women (and mothers) with shaky mental health. They're not delirious or weak. They're burnt out!

Having time to unwind isn't a nice to have, it's essential and many parents are deprived of this nowadays. Studies have proven how self-care can impact mental health in all regards, including:

- Reducing and even eliminating symptoms of depression and anxiety.
- Eliminating the effects of excess stress.
- Minimizing feelings of anger, resentment, and frustration.
- Increasing energy levels and general feelings of happiness.
- Heightening concentration levels and cognitive abilities.

I don't know about you, but I would rather be focusing on myself and my well-being than stretching myself so thin that I hardly have time to enjoy any of the things that I used to enjoy – or my children, for that matter. Being alive and caring for yourself is costly enough as it is and I mean this in every aspect of the word. From material expenses to the toll that parenthood takes on your health, that is one expensive journey I don't wish to embark on. If that makes me selfish in the eyes of people who don't know anything about my goals, plans, or life in general, then so be it. That is honestly no skin off my back anymore and I hope that this will give other women the strength to feel that way too.

My life; my finances; my body; my choice. Period.

Chapter 5

Time to Focus on Your Career

For many people, having a successful career is a top priority in life. For those who have decided not to have children, the freedom to focus solely on their careers can bring a great sense of joy and fulfillment.

One of the greatest benefits of not having children is the ability to fully dedicate oneself to their career goals. Without the responsibility of raising children, individuals have more time and energy to focus on their work, hone their skills, and pursue career opportunities. This can lead to greater career success, higher salaries, and more professional satisfaction. I know it might sound like corporations across the globe have hired me to write a book that will convince everyone to be more productive and forget about family life, but I can assure you that this isn't true. Some people just prefer working towards tangible goals as opposed to gambling on whether they have what it takes to raise a sufficiently functional human being. Call us crazy if you want to, but that's what gets us up in the morning.

Knowing that I don't have to pass up a promotion with more responsibilities or overlook the possibility of being transferred to another one of my employer's locations keeps me smiling. I have made one difficult choice that has saved me thousands of other difficult choices. I have no desire to be responsible for anyone else's stability but my own and I think more people would be better off if they began owning their inner beliefs instead of trying to conform.

Not having children can indeed provide a greater sense of control over one's career because of the ability to structure their time and work location in a way that works best for them. If the option is available to me, being able to work from home on most days and heading to the office on maybe 2-3 days of the week would work well for me. I wouldn't lose any productive hours sitting in traffic and then regulating my nervous system for the first 30 minutes after I've stepped into the office. I can stay home, enjoy the silence, keep my home clean, and be more productive. I would be winning all around. Trying to work with children in the house is nigh on impossible. Just ask a handful of parents that had to do this during the global lockdowns that occurred in 2020.

There are some career opportunities that are once-in-a-lifetime deals. Being able to attend an impromptu meeting with an important client on behalf of my boss, taking over some of their duties while they're on vacation, or even walking away from a toxic work environment to establish my own business are all possibilities for me without a child to care for. Of course, it's important to note that not having children doesn't necessarily guarantee career success or personal fulfillment. Everyone's path is different, and some individuals may find that they are happiest when balancing both work and family responsibilities. Moreover, just because you don't have children that doesn't automatically mean that you're going to become some massive success in the near future or become the first (or next) millionaire in your family. However, for those who have chosen not to have children, the ability to focus solely on their career can be a great source of joy and fulfillment. Understanding the flexibility of one's work environment is critical. Some roles are not easily replaced and, as such, if you are replaced after a prolonged stay at home with a child, you could potentially lose your position. While discrimination against pregnant women and new mothers is considered illegal in most parts of the world, there are corporations and small businesses alike that are crafty enough to rid themselves of what they will see as a burden. Is this uncouth and disgusting behaviour? Absolutely. Is it a reality for many women around the world nonetheless? You bet it is!

With all of that in mind, I like to make sure I have a retort for some of the quips that I can see arising from my research and personal take on being childless. This chapter will be no different. So, here's one for you. People might say that some parents actually find joy in coming home to their screaming children at the end of the day and that they serve as a wonderful distraction from their "real problems". To that I say, your children shouldn't be a distraction. If you're having children to distract yourself from any aspect of your life, there is something seriously wrong that you're not addressing. For another thing, you can't refute statistics. The stats are in and they show that the vast majority of empty nesters – those are people between the ages of 50 and 75 – are far happier than their younger counterparts who still have children living at home with them. In fact, their happiness quotient rapidly increases from the moment their kids leave the nest! [24]

You can't argue with the data.

Freedom of Movement

For the first few years of your child's life, you're not going to be able to make any concrete plans in advance unless you have that solid village that we discussed earlier. Your movements will be very limited and even leaving the room where your sleeping child is asleep will become an extreme sport. If you can't see yourself slithering off the edge of a bed while staring at your newborn and praying that you don't make a sound in the process, you're not ready for parenthood. If you can't imagine crawling out of your toddler's bedroom like a ninja and getting up 2-5 times a night to get them back to bed when you begin sleep training, then perish the parenting thought. Are you thinking that co-sleeping might work in your favour? Then you can kiss having alone time with yourself – or your partner – in the evening hours goodbye until your child is a pre-teen.

Simply put, your movements become restricted. Just leaving the city, state, or country without your child can send you down a spiral of mom guilt that is enough to stop you in your tracks. Yes, there are women that simply get on with it, but many of us just don't want that on our shoulders. Imagine planning the perfect getaway and paying for it only for your child to come down with a fever the night before. You'd have to try to postpone the trip but, in many instances, your bookings would not be refunded because of the fact that you'll have attempted to postpone or cancel them on such short notice. I understand that there are worse things that could potentially happen to a person and I'm sure there are parents out there who would see the silver lining (thank goodness Jimmy* didn't show signs after we had already left), but I'll say it again: this is not for everyone.

Someone might say that those years are fleeting and I'm sure that they are, but what do you do in all the years after that period ends; when you want to travel alone but can't? How about when you want to travel with your kids, but it becomes such a hassle as we looked at earlier? Traveling with children is never easy, and it requires a lot of planning and preparation. Parents have to worry about packing all the necessary items for their child, such as diapers, formula, clothes, toys, and more. They also have to worry about their child's safety and well-being during travel, which can be stressful and overwhelming. Additionally, parents may have to avoid certain destinations that are not child-friendly or require long flights, which can limit their options for travel.

Another way that having children restricts your movements is through leisure activities. Parents often have to give up their favorite hobbies or activities that are not suitable for children or cannot be done with them. For example, parents may not be able to participate in extreme sports, attend concerts or events late at night, or even go out for a quiet dinner without worrying about the child's safety and long-term well-being. Even simple activities such as going to the movies or shopping can become challenging with a child in tow.

Parents also have to be careful about their social life and interactions with others. They may not be able to attend social gatherings or events that are not suitable for children, or they may have to leave early if the child becomes fussy or uncomfortable. Even visiting friends or family members may become a challenge, as parents have to bring their children with them and follow them around to make sure they're not breaking anything. I can't tell you how many mothers I've witnessed juggling their children while trying to eat a meal or just have a sip of their drink. During the infant period, parents haul their entire house with them to make sure they have enough spare diapers, clothes, and emergency care supplies to make sure that they don't have to head back home mid-outing. In the toddler years, they have to prevent a tiny human from harming themselves and those tiny humans seem hellbent on doing that very thing. In the childhood years, there is some semblance of calm but there are still restrictions. Then the teen years hit and it becomes a juggling act of emotions as well as wanting to go out of town and trust your teen at home (if you live somewhere safe enough for this and they are of age). This is opposed to sitting tight until they're adults because you don't want to come back home to your teen's version of a frat party in your home.

Whichever way you spin it, parents have tough choices to make with regards to their movements. The freedom of going where you want, with whom you want, and for how long you want to is priceless.

Financial Independence

Deciding whether to pay for hockey practice and all the gear that goes with it or to buy myself a new winter outfit (or a couple of them – depending on where you shop) is not a decision I want to have to be making. Having to check in with what my children have going on before I can give myself to spend a dime of my hard-earned money doesn't sound like an enjoyable time to me.

In Sweden, for example, it costs €189,100 [25] to raise a child from birth until the age of 18. Add another 10 years if the current trend of arrested development in some regions and unemployment in other regions continues, and you'll be spending a whole lot more than that. In America, on the other hand, it can cost €15,000 per year [26] to raise a child depending on the state and city that a person lives in. That's €240,000 over 18 years and that's not even factoring in inflation.[6] Just think about a person's earning trajectory and whether they would ever be able to catch up with expenses if they had a child prematurely (or at all) where finances are concerned.

---

[6] Averages are true as of the year of writing this book. Subject to change with time.

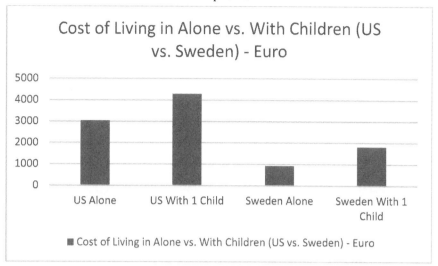

Figure 3: Expenses in Euros With & Without Children (USA & Sweden)

While the financial leap between childlessness and having children isn't that large in some countries, it almost doubles in others. Considering the cost of living in some countries, doubling expenses is not something that many adults in their so-called "prime childbearing years" care to do. Nobody wants to live in a begrudging state. Nobody wants to think that they would be better off if only they were single and childless. And while there are countless healthy relationships with individuals who have zero regrets about having children from a financial standpoint, there are just as many who do have those regrets.

I've got one life. We all do. Childless people have just chosen financial independence (amongst many other benefits) over having children. It isn't the worst thing in the world. I would even go so far as to say it is the right thing to do in many circumstances because it shows restraint, discipline, and a sense of responsibility towards oneself and those around them.

Plus, could you imagine running into a medical emergency in countries where public healthcare isn't what it should be and not having the funds to help yourself or your child? The thought is heart-wrenching. At the risk of sounding like someone who doesn't take risks (see what I did there), trust me, I do. I just prefer logical and calculated risks over throwing caution to the wind.

A Healthier You & Healthier Relationships

Stress is a silent killer and studies show that parents are more stressed than their childless peers. In fact, mothers are 40% more stressed than fathers or their childless peers. [27] Guess what was the only way suggested to possibly help them combat this level of stress? Wait for it – the solution that was suggested was for them to cut back on work outside of the home. For women who don't have that luxury or want that lifestyle, their only choice is to be childless or to be more stressed.

I'll take being less stressed. Childless people are more "Zen" and one reason for this is that they tend to have more time for self-care. Without the demands of raising children, they have more time to focus on their physical and mental health. They can prioritize things like regular exercise, healthy eating, and getting enough sleep. They can take time off work when they need to without having to worry about childcare responsibilities, which will ultimately be waiting for them from the very first day of their vacation period. Plus, without the financial burden of raising kids, people without children may have more resources to invest in their own health and well-being. If you're sick, you only have to worry about one consultation, one set of meds, and one person. If you have children, go ahead and start multiplying the costs. Moreover, you might be able to afford healthier food, gym memberships, or even therapy, thus skipping the potential of dread diseases altogether.

People without children may also have less exposure to germs and illnesses. Kids are notorious for bringing germs home from school and daycare, which can spread quickly throughout the household. Add this to a parent's lack of sleep and the increased stress that comes with raising children and you'll have one seriously weakened immune system.

So, now you're home sick with a child who is home sick, your partner is annoying you, they've bought the wrong meds for the baby (who caught your toddler's cold like you did) and you want to snap. Now, your mental health is on the brink too! Mental health is another area where people without children may have an advantage. While having children can bring immense joy and fulfillment, it can also be a significant source of stress and anxiety. Parents may worry about their children's safety, health, and future, and the responsibility of raising children can be overwhelming at times. People without children, on the other hand, may have more freedom to focus on their own mental health. They can also nip problems within their romantic relationship in the bud. They don't have to grumble under their breath and allow their anger to fester before they find an opportune, kid-free arena to have an uninterrupted adult conversation with their partner.

To cut a very long story short, you will not be consumed by the demands of raising children and will be free to prioritize your relationships with your partners, family, and friends. Why? Well, when people are happy and fulfilled, they are better able to be present and engaged in their relationships.

Research also suggests that people without children may have better communication skills and emotional intelligence. They have more time to reflect on their own emotions and needs, and this can help them to better understand and empathize with others. Additionally, without the added stress of raising children, they may be better able to manage their emotions in a more stable way and communicate effectively in their relationships. This, ultimately, makes for more intentional partnerships that aren't just continued because one or both parties are too tired to consider whether the fit is still correct. Without the expectation of having children to bond them together, people might also be more selective about the people they choose to spend time with and the kind of relationships they want to have.

*

I've always said that the benefits of being childless far outweigh the drawbacks. It doesn't matter much to me whether people believe that those with families live longer. Quality of life should be considered not just quantity or length. Sure, people with children might live longer, but it could be out of sheer will to stay alive for the sake of their predecessors. Maybe they need to stay alive longer because the constant interruptions stop them from reaching their goals in the timeframe that childless people reach theirs. I'm perfectly fine with having a slightly shorter but completely peaceful and fulfilling life. There isn't a single one of us that is getting out of here alive, anyway.

CHAPTER 6 – HOW THE CHILDLESS PERSON BUILDS A FULFILLING LIFE

Before I delve into how the childless person builds a fulfilling life without children, I want to begin by giving you a toolkit to do the very same. Things are, therefore, about to take a different turn in this book as we shift gears once more from simply looking at facts and figures to walking through a few practical tips. Yes, the facts will still be peppered throughout the book because I know just how human beings can be. Apparently, without "hard" evidence from other human beings, we can't trust other human beings. (That's my punny take on the fact that we're all "others" to someone no matter what our title, by the way.)

I'll quit with the humour while I'm ahead.

Let's get back to the topic at hand: how you can build a fulfilling life as a childless person.

I believe that it all begins with two little P-words – passion and purpose. For the longest time, people have been told to give up on passion and just focus on becoming somewhat passionate about whatever job lands in their lap. I can see the logic in that. Everybody needs to eat and have shelter. These things cost money, so the rationale is that if your passion isn't paying the bills, it might be time to reassess your strategies.

This might be true...or you might just be looking at things from the wrong angle.

A Life of Passion

I'm well aware that you can pursue your passion when you have children but, more often than not, passion falls by the wayside and is almost instantly replaced with responsibilities when children are born. If you were prone to falling victim to peer pressure – including the pressure to have a child – you'll be prone to the prods from family members to "get a real job". Childbearing is often where the passionate dreams of drummers, painters, and ballerinas go to die.

Living a life of passion is often associated with following one's dreams, pursuing one's goals, and creating a meaningful existence. While some may assume that having children would limit one's ability to live such a life, the truth is that living a life of passion is achievable regardless of whether or not one has children. But, not having children may provide more opportunities to live a life of passion, as it allows for greater flexibility, freedom, and focus. Trying to follow one's passion while raising a child is difficult, to say the very least. This is especially true if your passion involves any of the aforementioned areas of expertise that might involve late-night performances, out-of-town exhibitions, and more. If your child falls ill or your childcare provider becomes indisposed, you might have to miss out on such events. If the events were established specifically to showcase you, that is going to be a serious wrench in the works. Now, people might say that you have just as much probability of falling ill before your big event as a child does, but that simply isn't true. Parents are 28% more prone to getting sick than adults who don't have children. [28]

So, yes, one of the most significant benefits of not having children is the freedom to pursue one's passions without child-related constraints on one's time, finances, and emotions. I want to be able to ask myself whether the career I'm currently in is really for me in the next 10 years – if need be, of course. What's more important is that I want to be able to do this without worrying whether my career change is going to impact my child's life. If you don't want to have to conduct a mammoth balancing act between your child's needs and pursuing your passion, then being childless might just be for you. Pursuing that spark that drives you can lead to a greater sense of fulfillment and satisfaction, as you can pour all of your energy and resources into what you enjoy.

This is tied closely to the ability to take risks and try new things. Childless individuals do not have to worry about the impact of their choices on their children's lives and can be more adventurous in their pursuits. Traveling abroad for the summer to take up a pastry course, thus, entertaining a dream of being a pastry chef is easier when you're childless than it is when you have children. Taking on challenging projects, traveling to new places for work, and exploring a different career path (or two) without being tied down by the responsibilities of parenting is a freedom like no other. Plus, if I'm ever not in a position to pursue my passions, I would much rather blame it on circumstances than on an innocent child who didn't ask to be born.

As a childless person, being able to maintain a sense of independence and autonomy is but one of the many ways that you will build a fulfilling life. Agency is the name of the game and having the wiggle room to pick a lifestyle and make decisions based solely on your own preferences and desires. If you're hoping to live a life with a greater sense of self-awareness and self-fulfillment, then continue focusing on building a life that is tailored to your own needs and wants. That way, you will build elements of your life that are of substance without worrying about the material or mental cost that comes along with that.

This will, ultimately, help you find your purpose.

Finding Your Purpose

Finding purpose and meaning without children is far easier if you ask me. Without the responsibility of raising a child, those who choose to remain childless have the opportunity to fully immerse themselves in their thoughts about their lives. You can perform as much mental gymnastics as you like while you think back to what you've always been passionate about and how you've been able to serve others around you. This is, after all, where you find your purpose: at the intersection of passion and service.

That's something that I feel many people miss the mark on. They equate their purpose with their passion alone and forget that purpose can be found in a life of service to others. This mustn't be confused with a life of servitude because service and servitude are not one and the same. Due to the fact that so many of us fly off into survival mode when we have children – particularly those who have experienced consistent trauma – we tend to focus solely on our own needs and the needs of our children. However, when you have the freedom to connect with others and serve them, this can lead to breakthroughs in terms of your purpose and, perhaps, your career. You might just come up with the next great app or invention that fills the needs of others and helps you step into a purposeful career. To be frank, when you don't have children, you have the freedom to choose how you spend your time and can pursue any passion that strikes your fancy. Whether it's writing a book, starting a business, or pursuing a new hobby, the world is your oyster.

If you want to take a pottery class, go ahead! If you want to go back to school to become a veterinarian, you can do that too! Without all of the unforeseen expenses that come along with raising children and the uncertainty in your schedule, you can set targets and stick to them – targets that will help you accumulate the finances necessary to take a class or switch your entire career. Immersing yourself in those moments that are delectably yours and yours alone will set you up to find your purpose.

The question is, once you're in those moments, how do you find your purpose?

In my personal opinion, The first step to finding your purpose is to reflect on your values and beliefs. Think about what matters most to you, and what you stand for. Your values are the guiding principles that inform your decisions and actions. Write down a list of your core values and beliefs, and think about how they can be integrated into your daily life.

Identifying how those values align with your passions and interests will be an integral step. Working in a manner that sits outside the boundaries of what you believe to be morally in line with your values will only leave you feeling worn out and depleted. There is such a thing as mental depletion, which is basically just a fancy way of saying you've been doing too much that is too far outside the realm of what sits well with your soul for far too long.

Once you've aligned all of those elements, reflect on your strengths and talents. Your strengths are the things that you are naturally good at, and your talents are the skills that you have developed over time. I have to make sure that you clearly understand the difference between the two because talent is not innate. It can be honed. In other words, if you've always dreamt of skateboarding, you can learn how to do so no matter how old you are. Sure, you might break a few more bones than a child would and it might take you a little longer to learn, but you can still hone this skill. In fact, let's start using the word skill instead of talent.

Moving on. Make a list of your strengths and talents and think about how they can be applied to your daily life. Consider how you can use your strengths and talents to make a positive impact on the world. If you're stumped for ideas on how to make a positive impact on the world or the thought is just far too overwhelming to contend with, start small. How can your strengths and skills help your neighbour or someone in your community? Even if you can serve just one person, you'll be able to:

a. Develop your purpose, or,
b. Find your real purpose.

The problem is, how would you know which person on your street or in your community could do with your service? Volunteering and giving back to the community are great ways to figure this out. Volunteering allows you to help others and make a positive impact, all while gaining new skills and experiences that can be applied to your personal and professional life. Look for volunteer opportunities that align with your truest interests and values. Check out the bulletin boards around the city and look for Facebook groups that are specifically for your community to start turning those mental gears and generating new ideas.

Sometimes, finding your purpose requires stepping outside of your comfort zone and trying new experiences. Experimenting with where you go, what you do, and who you meet up with will give you a better understanding of your likes and dislikes. This is super important for anyone who was raised in a very controlling household because you might just be walking around with a set of likes and dislikes that do not apply to you. It can also help you discover new passions and interests. If you're struggling with this, think about mentorship.

A mentor can provide guidance and support as you navigate your journey to finding your purpose. Seek out a mentor who has experience in your existing or preferred field. They'll be able to offer you advice, feedback, and encouragement – simultaneously keeping you accountable with your goals and holding space for you in your difficult moments. They can also provide insights into their own journey and help you avoid common pitfalls. From there, I would greatly recommend partaking in self-reflection and mindfulness as it will help you gain clarity and perspective on your journey to finding your purpose. Practice mindfulness techniques such as meditation and deep breathing to help you gain clarity. Similarly beneficial are practices such as yoga. Set aside time each day for self-reflection, whether it's journaling, practicing gratitude, or simply taking a walk in nature. If that isn't for you and it sounds like your idea of a nightmare, then you can try activities that allow your brain to focus on one activity at a time, such as building puzzles or doing crosswords. For people with incredibly active minds, having something that doesn't require them to sit still in silence is better than – well – sitting still in silence.

Once you have identified your purpose, set goals and take action to achieve them. This may involve writing your goals down and breaking them down into manageable steps or milestones.

Always remember that finding your purpose, like anything else, takes time and you should celebrate your wins along the way.

Focus on Personal Aspirations

Childless people have the time to question what they want out of life and actually pursue avenues that can answer that question. This falls somewhere along the lines of finding your purpose and pursuing your passion. While passions are more often linked to career paths and activities of that nature, aspirations are more often linked to things that we want to pursue just for the sake of pursuing them. The simple joy of pursuing something and the hope of being able to pursue it is what makes something an aspiration.

Recent studies indicate that parents often set their aspirations aside and replace them with aspirations for their children's lives. [29] This becomes potentially detrimental for both the child in question as well as the parents because parents can begin to project all of their childhood programming, hopes, and dreams onto their children. That spells disaster. A child who feels as though they have something to prove to their parents and who feels as though they always need to try their best to live up to those expectations will be wildly unhealthy. They will develop a perfectionism complex and this will leave them feeling burnt out. They will become a version of themselves that feels foreign and unrecognizable to them, putting them at risk for adverse mental health and, in severe cases, premature death via suicide.

Yeah, that's not something I want to ever feel responsible for. I don't know about you, but I have my own aspirations to focus on – aspirations that I do not want to project onto a child just because I had them before I had the chance to see certain things through. For those who have always had a dream career or wanted to pursue a specific aspiration, not having children can provide the opportunity to focus on that goal without distractions. They can work long hours or take on extra projects without worrying about the impact on their family or childcare responsibilities. This level of focus and dedication can often lead to greater success and satisfaction in one's career or personal pursuits. While I'm not promoting that level of somewhat abhorrent productivity to become the norm for the childless person, it is possible to burn the midnight oil when need be and to do so completely guilt-free.

Of course, the decision to not have children does not necessarily mean a life devoid of responsibilities. Childless individuals may still have aging parents, pets, or community obligations that require time and attention. More importantly, we have ourselves to take care of! Yes, a life of service is great, but let's not act like taking care of and prioritizing ourselves is some sort of "sin".

While there are many benefits to being childless and pursuing personal aspirations, it is important to note that this path is not without its challenges. You will need to create a routine and dig deep to find discipline. If you don't, you could fall into the trap of procrastination or a lack of direction.

Hobbies to Fill Your Days

It's important to be able to engage in hobbies that can take your mind off of work stress, relationship issues, and any other mentally draining aspects of life. The caveat for couples with children is obviously that one partner often gets to lean into this area of their lives more than the other. While there are couples who can drop their kids off with their parents and enjoy their hobbies individually or as a couple, not everyone has that luxury.

And let's not pretend like hobbies aren't just as important to some people as other aspects of their daily lives.

Hobbies are not just a way to pass the time, but they can also bring many benefits to our mental and physical health. Engaging in a hobby can help you relax and unwind after a long day or week, reset your mind, and reduce stress levels. In fact, studies have shown that certain hobbies can even help you live longer by reducing the risk of developing chronic diseases such as heart disease, stroke, and dementia.

Finding a hobby that suits you can be challenging, but it's worth the effort. First off, you'll be able to relax your mind. Engaging in an activity that you enjoy can help you forget about the stresses of daily life and immerse yourself in something that brings you joy. Whether it's reading a book, painting, gardening, or playing an instrument, taking time to do something that you love makes life that much richer and more meaningful.

Hobbies can also help you reset your mind for the week ahead. Many people find that engaging in a hobby on the weekends or after work on weekdays can help them feel refreshed and ready to tackle the week ahead. The level of activity that you engage in will possibly be equivalent to the level of stress that you've faced during the week. If you find it harder to switch your mind off, more rigorous sporting hobbies may be in order. However, if you just want to spend time doing something that you enjoy and don't feel the need to get physical in order to turn your mental chatter off, then just about anything will do.

Hobbies can, therefore, be an excellent way to reduce stress levels because of the release of dopamine (our feel-good chemical) that occurs during activities that are worthwhile to us. You'll elevate your brain's sense of control over its environment and make it feel more commanding in the moment. This is all while you continue to trigger your brain's reward center and release dopamine.

The bonus is that engaging in an activity that you enjoy can help you feel happier and more satisfied with life as the sense of accomplishment associated with hobby participation deepens.

Creating Relationships of Significance

This is going to be a common theme in this book because those who push the agenda of every woman on earth having children also tend to push the idea that one benefit of this is the relationship that is built with her child. However, you can create relationships of significance whether you have children or not. In fact, you might build relationships that are of more significance because you, as well as the people in your life, have chosen to be in one another's lives. It might sound awful, but you can't be certain of what type of person your child is going to grow up to be. You don't know for sure whether they're going to constantly call you to bail them out of trouble. You don't know if that relationship is going to enrich your life or stress you out. The same goes for your partner. You've never had a child with them before, so how do you know whether or not they're going to be a good parent? How do you know whether or not they're going to switch up their personality or behaviour on you after your first child is born?

Chapter 6

Whether people like to admit it or not, not having children allows for more time to build connections with friends, colleagues, and mentors. The decision to forego parenthood provides ample opportunities to cultivate deeper relationships that can last a lifetime.

Being childless frees up a significant amount of time to focus on relationships with friends. This can lead to stronger, deeper, and more meaningful connections. I've seen my fair share of friends – even lifelong friends – who have fallen out of one another's lives after one (or both) had children. And the relationship never went back to the way that it was before having children; even after the children were older, off to school, and presumably less stressful or time-consuming. We've placed such importance on romantic relationships and the traditional family unit that we fail to see the importance of genuine friendships. You can argue that the people I mentioned (the ones who fell out after having children) were never really friends, to begin with, but I beg to differ. They've just been programmed to believe that their marriage and relationship with their child should take precedence over every other relationship in their lives and, in some cases, they've had unsupportive spouses or partners who don't value their friendships either.

The simple fact is that, without the demands of raising a family, childless individuals are able to plan social events and gatherings, take impromptu trips, and be available to provide emotional support for their friends when needed. This availability fosters deeper and more consistent relationships. I will say that there are just as many people who have amazing friendship bonds after having children and their children grow up to be friends too, but these people are a rarity. Even if you are fortunate enough to fall into this category, you might not have time for mentors, peers, or colleagues, who can help you develop your career-related skills and networks. Your ability to hang back after work and grab a beer (or mocktail) with colleagues in order to pick their brains and seek advice cannot be underestimated. When you're isolated at work and feel like you're not a part of the social circle within the office, you might begin to feel anxious around your peers. Mild delusions can set in and you might start to think that they don't like you or are speaking ill of you in your absence.

Finally, there are the relationships with siblings and parents. If they aren't on your back about having children and aren't bringing toxicity or negativity into your life, not having children in the midst of these relationships can make them all the more rewarding in adulthood. The joy of moving from being a child to a companion within your family dynamic is truly something to behold and you will not be disappointed that you waited or opted to forego having children altogether.

The Joy of Nothingness

Being able to have days where you simply relish in your existence without having to do anything productive to feel worthy of life is incredible. Il dolce far niente is an Italian phrase that was popularized by the film rendition of Elizabeth Gilbert's book, *Eat, Pray, Love: One Woman's Search for Everything Across Italy, India and Indonesia*. It is a firm favourite for many people because of the meaning behind it. Loosely translated, il dolce far niente means "the sweetness of doing nothing".

In today's society, the pressure to constantly be productive and achieve success can be overwhelming. Do you know what that constant pressure gets you? It gets you a bad case of burnout, stress, and even physical, as well as mental, health problems. However, for those who choose to be childless, there is an opportunity to embrace the joy of doing nothing and not having to be productive all the time. Have a look at the next figure. You'll see how some of the happiest countries in the world have the shortest workweeks.

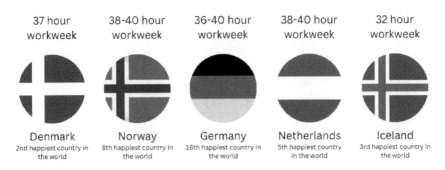

Figure 4: Happiest Countries & Their Work Hours[7]

One of the benefits of being childless is the freedom to embrace a slower pace of life. Rather than constantly rushing to meet the demands of parenting, childless individuals can take the time to do things they enjoy and prioritize their mental and physical well-being. This allows for the opportunity to disconnect and recharge, which is essential for maintaining good health and preventing burnout.

Taking time to do nothing also provides the opportunity to be present in the moment. With a slower pace of life, individuals can fully engage in experiences without feeling rushed or distracted. This can lead to a greater appreciation for life and the

---

[7] Data from World Population Review: https://worldpopulationreview.com/country-rankings/happiest-countries-in-the-world

simple pleasures it has to offer. In fact, some people might consider this the ultimate form of mindful living – one where you don't have to practice all these different types of meditations and mindfulness just to keep up with the rampant demands on your psyche.

In addition to being beneficial for mental and physical health, doing nothing can also enhance creativity and productivity. Research has shown that taking breaks and allowing the mind to wander can increase creativity and improve problem-solving skills. This will give you a greater sense of inner peace and contentment. In a world that is constantly on the go, taking the time to slow down and enjoy life can feel like a brazen fight against the status quo as you work on developing balance and harmony.

Of course, it's important to note that there is a difference between taking the time to do nothing and being unproductive or lazy. It's simply a matter of taking the time to just be. We're not meant to suffer through life. We're meant to enjoy life without the constant pressure to be productive all the time.

*

There are many more ways that childless people build fulfilling lives. I could have written an entire book on that subject alone. However, these are some of the ways that stand out to me and I'm sure this goes the same for many others. With time, people can eventually begin to accept the fact that being childless is a personal choice. However, this is more so for single women than it is for couples. This is why we must excavate the societal issues that abound in the childless couple conundrum.

CHAPTER 7 – THE CHILDLESS COUPLE CONUNDRUM

C hildless couples have their own set of challenges and opportunities to contend with. Society sees a couple and their minds immediately turn to questions such as:

- *Are they married?*
- *Do they live together?*
- *Are they just dating?*
- *Are they friends with benefits?*
- *Are they even in a relationship?*
- *Do they have children?*
- *Do they intend on having children?*
- *Why haven't they had any children yet?*

If some people could, I really believe that they would ask whether or not a couple had sex before they left the house that morning. To me, and many others, this is literally how bold and tactless it comes off when a person asks about someone's familial status.

That said, it's often the tone in which this is implied that can make matters worse for the opposing party in the eyes of the childless couple. Body language, facial expressions, tone of voice, and persistence are often the real issue. The situation in which the questions are asked must also be considered. Some instances can be forgiven, as we looked at when we began this deep dive.

Someone at the reception desk of an island resort asking a couple if they're on honeymoon or making statements about lots of babies being made on their resort is, in my opinion, harmless small talk. I'll most likely never see that person again. However, it's a different story if an in-law glares at you as they indignantly ask, "What's wrong with my child then? Planning on leaving him/her?"

Nevertheless, whether it comes from perfect strangers or family members, the pressure always intensifies when you're in a committed relationship.

The Pressure Intensifies

People will ask the question more often if you're in a relationship. The societal pressure to have children is a topic that has been discussed for decades. It seems that as soon as you reach a certain age or get married, people start asking when you will have children. This pressure can be particularly intense for women, who are often expected to have children and become mothers.

Firstly, marriage is often seen as the first step towards starting a family. The traditional model of a family is a married, heterosexual couple with children, and this is still deeply ingrained in our society. When people get married, it is often assumed that they will start trying to have children soon after. This assumption is so deeply ingrained that it is often not even questioned. What makes this incredibly toxic is that many people are of the belief that a couple cannot be a family. Single mothers or single fathers who live alone with their children are likely to also suffer the same folly of wanton commentary. We have this programming in our minds of what a family should look like and we tear down the beautiful togetherness of others simply because it doesn't fit into our idea of what a family should be. A happily married couple is a family. A mother and her child are a family. Grandparents and their once-orphaned grandchildren are a family. Three best friends and their pug are a family. Family is the blood of the covenant. It is the tribe that we choose when we no longer have to be tied to the water of the womb should we choose not to be.

For some odd reason, marriage is often seen as a sign of maturity and responsibility. It is assumed that once you get married, you are ready to take on the responsibilities that come with being a parent. This assumption can be particularly strong for women, who are often expected to put their own desires and ambitions on hold in order to become mothers. What's even more odd is that if you live with your partner in blissful harmony without being married or get married and choose not to have children, you're seen as contrary to the first statement. In other words, you're painted as an immature and selfish person.

Why? Why is there this societal belief that having children is the ultimate goal in life? Why is this something that we should all aspire to? Many people believe that having children is the key to happiness and fulfillment and that those who do not have children are somehow incomplete or missing out on something important. This belief is often reinforced by the media, which tends to portray families with children as the ideal. Everywhere you look, there are adverts that are geared towards the traditional family setup. Don't even get me started on how those adverts are mostly racially inclined, depicting same-race couples and perpetuating stereotypes that harm people of colour.

The pressure to have children can be particularly intense for women, who are often judged more harshly than men for not having children. The fact that we're seen as selfish, immature, or even unnatural for not wanting to have children ostracizes us as if we're social pariahs. Just as children are most often harmed by those closest to them, we're often ostracized by friends and family.

If you were born into a religious family or a family of a certain culture, not having children might come with severe consequences. It can be seen as disobedient or sinful and this can have dramatic implications on the relationship between the adult child and their family. It's borderline cultish!

But don't throw your family under the bus just yet because that cultish behaviour stems from how deeply ingrained it is in society. Look at the toys that are commonly given to young girls in comparison to those given to young boys. Baby dolls, ironing boards, and kitchen sets are what almost every young girl wants to have. Young boys are teased for wanting to play with dolls or kitchen sets and we wonder why women are struggling to find partners worth having children with – partners who don't know how to be nurturing with babies or prepare a meal while their wives are nursing. This isn't true for every household. People are becoming more modernized in their parenting approaches and are realizing the importance of gender neutrality in childhood.

That, however, isn't going to stop older generations from telling you that your way is wrong with a capital "W". If that pressure isn't for you and you'd rather remain childless, that's your choice to make.

Chapter 7

To Get Married or Not to Get Married

Earlier we looked at how a couple can be a family if they are married but do not have children. Now, I need to say that a couple can be a family regardless of whether they are married. Marriage is a huge step in anyone's life and despite the fact that it comes with a variety of benefits, it also comes with a variety of challenges. On one hand, marriage can offer stability, companionship, and support, but on the other hand, it can also bring expectations and pressure from society. That said, let's look at some of the other benefits.

- Increased social security benefits.
- Increased ease of buying a home with joint finances.
- Increased probability of income tax breaks.
- Enhanced simplicity in insurance planning and splitting.

As you can see, there is more to a marital partnership than just having children. Bringing a child into the world is possible whether or not a couple is married and, in a secure and trusting partnership, couples do not need a piece of paper to guarantee whether both parents will honour their commitments. When all is said and done, marriage is chock-full of benefits, but that doesn't mean anyone should feel obligated to get married. I would be remiss not to say that the aforementioned benefits are dependent on the part of the world that you live in and can be nationally, as well as regionally, specific.

These are more calculated in nature, so it's important to balance the benefits by looking at some of the more emotionally-inclined aspects of getting married. The emotional and psychological support that comes with having a life partner is incredible. Instead of having to be 100% solid on your own your entire life, you have someone to lean on during challenging periods in your life. Married couples are often able to rely on each other for comfort and encouragement, and studies have shown that married people tend to have better mental health outcomes than single people. But this depends on the quality of your marriage. Codependency could be a problem for couples and this could actually worsen the mental health issues of either partner. There is absolutely nothing that says you can't garner more support from a good friend than you do from a partner. A study of more than 270,000 people, spread across 100 countries, found that adult friendships are more important for health and well-being than relationships with family members. This increases in truth the older that we get as we tend to lean more on our friends for venting, advice, and guidance. [30]

While marriage can offer financial stability, as couples often pool their resources and work together towards shared financial goals, it's not for everyone. This is especially true if one partner tends to want to control situations. The often-difficult adjustment to merge two lives into one will become worsened by obsessive or controlling personalities. There may be conflicts and disagreements as each partner adjusts to the other's habits and quirks. In addition to this, marriage can bring added pressure from society and family to conform to certain expectations. One of the most prominent of these expectations is the pressure to have children.

There is a pervasive societal belief that marriage and children go hand in hand and that one of the main purposes of marriage is to produce offspring. This pressure can be particularly intense for women, which can lead to feelings of guilt, inadequacy, and shame for those who choose not to have children, or for those who are unable to have children for certain medical reasons.

Even for couples who do want children, the pressure to have them can still be overwhelming. There are often expectations about when couples should start trying to conceive, how many children they should have, and how they should raise them. The levels of stress and anxiety, particularly if the couple is facing fertility issues or is struggling to balance work and family life, can put a strain on a relationship and lead to its demise. If you include the expectation that couples should be deeply in love and devoted to each other at all times and that they should be each other's best friend and constant companion, you might want to run for the hills before you ever say "I do". There is also a belief that couples should have a shared sense of identity and purpose and that they should always be moving forward together towards a shared vision of the future. But some people are perfectly fine with just being companions without enmeshing every single fiber of their daily lives. This comes back to antiquated norms and stereotypes that are often (not always) perpetuated by older generations and their personal, cultural, and religious beliefs.

While these expectations can be positive in some ways, they can also be limiting and unrealistic. Not every couple is going to fit neatly into these boxes, and there is often a lot of pressure to conform to societal norms even if they don't align with one's personal values or desires. This can lead to feelings of isolation and disconnection, as well as a sense of being trapped in a relationship that may no longer be fulfilling or healthy.

Next thing you know, your partner will want to flip the script on you because of this societal pressure and that's when the tightrope that you've been walking begins to sway in the wind.

Chapter 7
When One Partner Changes Their Mind

Deciding whether or not to have children is a major life choice, and it's not uncommon for one partner in a relationship to change their mind about the matter. This can lead to a significant fallout that can affect both parties and their relationship.

When one spouse changes their mind about having a child, it can cause a rift in the marriage. The partner who wants a child may feel that their dreams and desires for the future are being disregarded, while the other partner may feel that they are being forced into a life-changing decision that they are not ready for or interested in. This can create feelings of resentment, disappointment, and even betrayal. What comes next can only be likened to a catastrophic implosion of emotions that then explodes outward and kills off any love or mutual respect as quickly and spectacularly as a dying star. This is because if the couple cannot come to an agreement on the matter, it can lead to a breakdown in communication and a loss of trust. In some cases, it can even lead to divorce. This is especially true if one partner feels that they were misled or that the other partner changed their mind after making a commitment to a certain life plan.

The wanting party will have to face the music at that stage because some people just don't do well with change at that level. There are several factors that can contribute to one spouse changing their mind about having a child. One of the most common is simply a change in priorities. As people grow and mature, their goals and desires for the future may shift. What was once a priority may no longer be as important, or a new desire may emerge. This can happen gradually over time or suddenly and unexpectedly.

On the other end of that spectrum, a change of heart can come about due to a shift in circumstances. For example, a change in career or financial situation may make one partner feel that they are not in a position to have a child when they had agreed on having children when the relationship first got underway. Alternatively, a significant event such as a health scare or the loss of a loved one may cause one partner to reassess their priorities and goals.

Regardless of the reason for the change of heart, it's important for both partners to communicate as openly and honestly with one another as possible. This means being willing to listen to each other's concerns and desires and being open to compromise. It's also important to recognize that there is no right or wrong answer when it comes to having children. Each person's desires and goals for the future are valid and should be respected. Remember to assess your relationship and where you stand as a couple. Don't allow broodiness and a sense of longing to drive you to make a decision that is going to be more permanent than a tattoo.

If the need arises, a trained therapist can help you explore your change in feelings and desires. This will help you work to find a solution that is satisfactory for both you and your partner. As a matter of fact, you might want to consider seeking therapy before you get married or before you consider settling on your joint decision of whether or not you should have children. Sometimes, having an intermediary in the room can help you say things that you might not have admitted to in the privacy of your own home. What's great about this is that you'll be able to do so in a manner that is amicable and that allows both of you – as partners – to fully understand one another.

The Antithesis

The childless couple is often seen as the antithesis, or the polarity, of the couple with children. This means that the childless couple can also appear to be a threat to the couple with children in the same way that a single, childless woman is a threat to the older, mother or matriarch-type figure. This is because of doubt. In the same way that the older woman once questioned whether she would have been better off alone, the married couple with children also questions whether they would have been better off not having children.

The thought can be enraging for some and they won't even understand why. They might think childless couples are a bunch of deviants who like to get up to sordid deeds on their own. They might think that their spouse will soon realize that they're not worth the stress and dump them with the kids before disappearing into the night.

All these doubts and insecurities come creeping in.

What I'm getting at is the fact that couples who choose not to have children can face criticism and judgment from those who have children, and this can lead to feelings of resentment and even hostility. For some, having children is a validation of one's life choices. They see it as a natural and necessary step in their life journey and they may struggle to understand why anyone would choose to live without children. If you want to know what superiority complexes look like, this is it, right here. Superiority complexes, if you were wondering, are linked to a deep-seated insecurity, and, here, the insecurity is probably tied to that validation. Couples who have children may feel that their decision to have children has been invalidated by couples who choose not to. They may feel that their sacrifice and hard work in raising children are not being recognized or appreciated by those who do not have children. It sounds bizarre, but we can draw those conclusions subconsciously because of the fact that we are creatures of metaphor. We create stories, metaphors, and analogies in our minds to make sense of the world around us. It's how we teach children to memorize certain things and this continues subconsciously into adulthood. So, yes, couples with children – as well as those without children – can draw conclusions from one another's choices as we see our opposites as mirror reflections of ourselves.

Couples who have children may wonder what their life would be like if they had chosen not to have children. They may worry that they are missing out on something or that they have made the wrong decision. Seeing couples who do not have children can be incredibly triggering, especially if there are doubts as to whether or not they've made the right decision in staying together or having children. This is an important point because how people react to your choices is almost certainly a reflection of how they feel about their own choices. If anyone is defensive and even aggressive about your decision to not have children, they might secretly be doubtful about their own decision to have children. While couples with children might be the ones judging couples without children, they may feel that they are being judged or criticized for their decision to have children. They may feel that they are being held to a higher standard of parenting or that their children are being analysed by couples who do not have children.

It's important to note that not all couples with children are going to feel this way. Remember, the whole point of this book is for us to break away from generalizations, not create more of our own.

If you're happily married and childless, it doesn't mean that your friends who are married with children need to be carved out of your life like next year's Halloween pumpkins.

The Positives are Limitless

Now let's look at some of the positives of being a childless couple, starting with the lewd elephant in the room. Sex is always on the table and it can happen just about anywhere in the house and at any time of day. There is just more time to enjoy one another as a couple on a multitude of levels. Two mature and healthy adults who are committed to living in harmony with one another don't need to outgrow the honeymoon phase. Sure, things won't always be as hot and heavy as they were in the early years, but choosing to be childless can help couples avoid relationship-ending challenges that often arise in parenthood. Childless couples enjoy a lower probability of divorce by comparison to their counterparts who have children – as can be seen below:

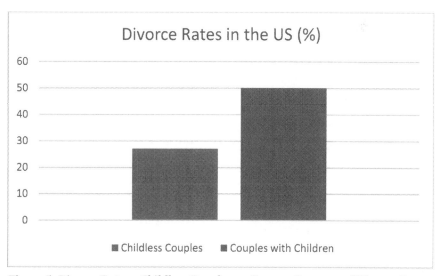

Figure 5: *Divorce Rates - Childless Couples vs. Parents Courtesy of <u>Divorce Source</u>*

I would rather be with someone for the rest of my life because I genuinely want to be with them, not just for the sake of sparing my children's feelings. When couples have more alone time, they have the opportunity to get to know each other on a deeper level. They may find that they enjoy spending time together and have a strong connection, or they may realize that they don't actually like each other as much as they thought.

It's no secret that having children changes your life. It brings new joys, new responsibilities, and new challenges. But for some couples, having children becomes the glue that holds their relationship together. Even if they're unhappy, they may feel that staying together is what's best for their children. This phenomenon is commonly referred to as "staying together for the kids." There are many reasons why couples may stay together for the kids. For some, it may be a fear of the unknown. They may not want to face the uncertainties of being single again, especially if they have been together for a long time. Others may worry about the impact that a divorce could have on their children. They may believe that their children need both parents to be present in their lives and fear that a divorce could disrupt this. Plus, divorce can be costly and it can be challenging to maintain the same standard of living after the fact. There is also a sense of duty that comes with being a parent. Many parents feel that it's their responsibility to put their children's needs before their own. This can make it difficult to leave a relationship, even if it's not fulfilling. This is why some couples with children are secretly unhappy most of the time. I believe that this is the predominant reason why studies show that the long-term happiness of childless couples is higher than that of couples with children.

Instead of adding to your expenses (yes, I know children are investments for the good of society), you could be using your funds to establish a business empire as a couple. Many couples today are choosing to focus on building successful businesses instead of having children. While starting a business can be a challenging and time-consuming endeavor, it can also be extremely rewarding and fulfilling. Without the expense of raising children, couples can invest more money into their business ventures and work towards greater financial stability and success. Building a business also provides couples with greater flexibility in their daily lives. They can set their own schedules and work from anywhere in the world, which can allow for more travel and opportunities to pursue other interests. For people with entrepreneurial blood in their veins, being childless might be the only way that they can fulfil this lifelong desire. For some couples, building a business together can provide a sense of purpose and fulfillment that may not come from having children. The satisfaction of building something from the ground up and seeing it succeed can be incredibly rewarding.

Just as parents want to leave a positive impact on their children, building a successful business can be a way for couples to leave a lasting legacy. However, building a business is, generally, less heartbreaking to deal with if things don't pan out according to plan. The idea of messing up another human being's ability to function versus potentially messing up a business is far more frightening. You can always start again with a business. You can open, close, sell, and buy as many businesses as you can afford to. You can't just start over with your children. Focusing on babies of the entrepreneurial kind can provide a sense of accomplishment and pride, as well as a way to give back to their community.

This is a great way to make a difference in the world, create jobs, donate to charitable causes, and use your business platform to raise awareness about issues that are important to you.

*

The childless couple is an anomaly according to society and they have always been seen as such. Men are chastised for not being "man enough". Women are lambasted for being prudes. There is no winning with some people. What is worth remembering is that no matter how much society piles on the pressure for you to have children, that is a decision between you and your partner alone. No one has a right to tell you when to have children or why just as they don't have a right to tell you what house to buy or what car to drive. These are personal decisions for a reason. The reason is that only you, as a couple, will have to live with those decisions for the foreseeable future.

CHAPTER 8 – REPLACING PRAMS WITH PLANES (OR TRAINS)

O ne of the best ways to ensure that you have a well-rounded life that is filled with an eclectic array of experiences as well as respect for people from all walks of life is to travel. Traveling broadens the mind and enriches the soul. It gives a person a sense of community and connection to the world around them. Whereas people who spend their entire lives in one place are more likely to fear the unknown, people who travel tend to be more open to the unknown. This, however, can't be said for people who are exposed to a multitude of cultures in an inbound fashion, such as people who live in areas that frequently receive high volumes of tourists.

Regardless of this, childlessness allows for more freedom and flexibility to explore the world.

I'm not saying that travel is not something that can be accomplished with children. There are many resorts and travel agencies that are focused on the family traveling experience. However, travel is currently not attainable for many of the average, working-class families around the world, the parents of which would likely be able to travel once a year if they were childless.

No, they shouldn't abandon their children in the pursuit of exploration and adventure, but it goes to show why generations that are now in their childbearing years are choosing to remain childless. We've reviewed the facts, we've seen firsthand how some families suffer just to get by, and we've decided that planes and trains are far more attractive to us than prams – or strollers.

There are so many options at our disposal in terms of work and travel nowadays and we owe it to ourselves to see where we fit in. To begin proving this point, enter stage right the digital nomad.

The Digital Nomads

The life of a digital nomad is becoming more and more desirable. The ability to travel the world while still earning an income and not being stressed about homeschooling or child safety in the process is a great way to broaden your mindset and meet new people. And here's a fun fact: it's easier to be a digital nomad without children than it is when you have children.

If you head to just about any social media platform, you can find hundreds of couples who are traveling the world with their children. You'll find the fliers, the mobile homers, and the backpackers – all of whom hit the skies, roads, or trails with their children all year round. It isn't impossible to achieve, but don't let social media fool you. Not everything that glitters is gold and there are a lot of "behind the scenes" issues that we're not aware of. Yes, you can head to your social media platform of choice and think that you can be a digital nomad parent, but if you have conflicting views on this, you're probably not going to have the best time. In other words, if you really want children and you believe that environmental stability is best for children, but you also really want to be a digital nomad and raise children of the world, one worldview will always supersede the other. Understanding why you feel the way that you do about being childless and committing to what works best for you should be your priority.

Circling back to the topic at hand, it's apparent that having children can prevent you from being a digital nomad. If you would rather move around without the constraints of a traditional 8-5 job, this might be a road (no pun intended) for you to go down. Considering that children need routine, stability, and familiarity to thrive, constant travel can disrupt their sense of security. If you don't have the mental fortitude and the type of calming or stoic energy that can give your child a secure sense of home no matter where they are, being a parent and a digital nomad is not advisable. If you do end up opting for the life of a digital nomad with children, you may need to stay in one place for longer periods of time, which can limit your ability to explore new destinations. Traveling with children requires careful planning, as parents need to ensure that their children have access to education, healthcare, and other essential services. This can be especially challenging in countries where these services are not easily accessible or are of poor quality. Additionally, traveling with children can be expensive, as parents need to pay for additional flights, accommodations, airport taxes, and other expenses.

Parents who want to be digital nomads may also struggle with the social aspect of traveling. Traveling can be a lonely experience, especially if you're a parent traveling with children. Meeting other digital nomads or local people can be difficult when you have children in tow, and it can be challenging to find other families who share your values and interests. This can make the digital nomad lifestyle feel isolating, which can be especially challenging for parents who are already dealing with the isolation that comes with raising children. The thought of that potentially turning into a new form of trauma for children makes it a newly unlocked fear that none of us need to deal with. And I get it – really,

I do. We don't need to be afraid of everything. There is no such thing as a perfect parent and we could all do without the neuroses of wondering whether or not we're actually parenting correctly should we decide to have kids. This is just my way of telling you that your options to do all of the amazing things that you want to do and having the freedom to do it completely of your own accord is not as attainable with children as it is without them.

I've thought about how digital nomads who have children might actually have it better because they're never truly lonely since they travel with their families. It honestly sounds good in theory, but all of the admin and logistics that go into traveling with children just for a week-long vacation tells me that it's not all sunshine and roses all of the time. Without knowing their surroundings well enough because of the fact that they're always strangers in a new foreign land, parents who are digital nomads will never have a break from one another or their children. As someone who values their personal space, I just don't think that would be for me or anyone else like me.

Gap Years & Sabbaticals

Let's use our imaginations again and assume that you were once a very ambitious person – maybe you still are – and you went straight from high school into university or college. Hey, you wouldn't even need to have been all that ambitious for that to happen! For most people who further their studies at a tertiary institution, there is no such thing as a gap year. This is particularly true for those who have won scholarships or partial funding for their studies and don't necessarily have the choice, or luxury, of taking a break to travel. When you don't have children, it's easier to take a break from work to focus on other professional pursuits or to just reassess your life. You have the time and likely the funds to do so. Now, let's say that you carried some, or all, of that young ambition through into your working years and have found yourself a well-paying job with flexible employers. But you've reached the fork in the road that many people do. Your options:

a. Keep on with your career.
b. Shake things up with a baby.

But you also have the opportunity to take that long-lost, and much-anticipated, gap year that you never got to take back when you graduated from high school. What are you going to do?

Sign me up for that gap year, especially if it's fully or even partially paid. This, my friends, is the gap year for professionals. It is the sabbatical.

Taking a sabbatical from work can be an incredible opportunity to recharge, refocus, and gain new perspectives. However, it can also be a daunting prospect, particularly for those with children, to worry about. When you have kids, there are numerous considerations that need to be taken into account, such as finding reliable childcare, ensuring that they are being well looked after, and keeping up with their school schedules. That is unless you want to do all of this yourself and travel around the block for the entire period of your sabbatical. If, on the other hand, you're taking a sabbatical and don't intend on traveling, you will still need to manage the household and your children's schedules instead of focusing on what you set out to achieve with this off-time. This can be a complicated and stressful process, and it can make it much harder to take extended time away from work.

Taking a sabbatical is something I recommend for anyone who has the opportunity to do so. It can be an incredibly enriching and rewarding experience, and it can help you to gain new perspectives, explore new interests, and learn more about yourself. If you're in a position to take time off from work for an extended period, but without pay, saving up for that period will be necessary. Without children in the picture setting a savings target and hitting your milestones consistently every month isn't just possible, it's probable. If you're a healthy adult without any medical issues that might eat into your savings and you're good at balancing a budget, this will be a cinch for you. You don't need to worry about feeling lonely or missing out on big events in your children's lives whether you'll be traveling for the entire sabbatical, furthering your studies abroad, or only being away from home for a portion of the sabbatical window. When you have children, this sense of isolation can be amplified, as you may feel guilty for leaving your kids behind or worry about what they are doing while you are away. Without children, however, you are free to fully immerse yourself in your sabbatical experience and make the most of the time you have.

I'm not here to tell the world that, all of a sudden, life is impossible to live once you have children. People have been getting on with life, focusing on their goals, and excelling in their careers with children in the mix literally since time immemorial. That isn't the point. I'm not trying to convert anyone to believe in childlessness as the ideal option for them. I'm only encouraging the people who have already made the choice and enlightening those who don't understand said choice. The sad truth is that parents probably need a sabbatical more than anyone else. Their lives have been so chaotic for so long that having the time to reassess would be beneficial to them. However, not every organization offers paid sabbaticals and taking one at the wrong time in life can eat into one's savings in nothing flat.

Travel is Less Expensive

Yes, this is something that we looked at briefly under the digital nomad section, but I want to dive into how traveling with children is mindbogglingly expensive whether you're doing it full-time, for a sabbatical, or just for a couple of days a year. This isn't spoken about enough and if you head to the website of any airline that you've recently used or a hotel that you once stayed at, you can request a quote to verify what I'm about to say. Ready? Here it goes.

Travel without children is less expensive!

The cost of airfare alone is eye-watering and it is often the same as the cost of airfare for adults, especially for children over the age of two. This can be a significant expense, particularly for long-haul flights. Furthermore, some airlines charge additional fees for families traveling with children, such as priority boarding, special seating, and additional weight fees for prams and booster chairs, which can be pretty heavy. This just further increases the cost of air travel and can be instantly off-putting. I know how I would feel if I saw an advert for flight specials, only to navigate to the site and be disappointed by how fast the costs add up with kids.

Other than the fact that you'll be paying for another human's flights so that they can tag along and explore everything with you, you'll also need to consider the number of rooms that you'll have to book. While some resorts offer family cabanas that are more affordable than some of their suites, most budget hotels will require that you book two separate rooms. Now, if your child isn't of the age to be in a hotel room by themselves, not only are you going to be paying double for accommodation, but you and your spouse will be no-contact at night for the duration of your stay. After all, one of you will have to be in the other room (even if it's adjoining) with your child.

Then there are the parents that are going to chime in and say that being away from their spouse for a couple of nights would actually be a welcomed break. That's because you're stressed out because of parenting and are going through phases of not being able to stand each other! But, hey, at least you're sticking together for the kids, right?

There is also everything else that goes into traveling with kids, such as picking a place that's safe for children, making sure you know where the nearest hospital is, and enquiring about pool safety (amongst other things) before you make your booking. You get the picture: traveling can be a costly endeavor, and the expenses can quickly add up, especially when traveling with children.

Eating out is another area where traveling with kids can be more expensive. Children have smaller appetites than adults, but they often want everything on the menu. Trying out a new restaurant could lead to a war between them wanting to order from the adult menu or them wanting more than one option from the kid's menu. Even though feeding them might be cheaper in theory, the fact that they often don't finish their meals (and then want a snack an hour later) will have you spending a small fortune on food while you're traveling. If you're planning on going to a country where the currency is stronger than your own and you have children, good luck to you! In contrast, couples and solo travelers can opt for less expensive dining options, such as street food or local markets, which can significantly reduce the cost of food. Sure, you might end up with food poisoning on your trip, but isn't that just a part of the experience?

I'm joking, of course. Take care of yourselves out there!

Speaking of taking care, transportation is another area where traveling with kids can be more expensive. Families may need to rent a larger vehicle, such as an SUV or minivan, to accommodate children and their luggage. If they haven't brought their booster chairs along, they might need to rent one. If they haven't thought ahead to see whether that's possible in the area that they're traveling to, they're either going to need to risk their children's safety or splash out on another set of booster chairs that they are then going to have to pay extra for on their flight home.

I ran out of breath just writing and reading over that last sentence.

It's a lot to grapple with.

If parents haven't completely broken the bank on food, flights, and accommodation, they might want to partake in some activities. These activities and attractions will come with ticket costs and admission fees for everyone involved. They can forget about quad biking, horse riding through the wilderness, bungee jumping, or white-water rafting. They're going to be in kiddy pools and on teacup rides. In contrast, couples and solo travelers can choose activities that are more affordable and may have more options available to them. They don't need to sell their souls to head to a certain famous resort that was popularized by a certain fictional mouse. (That's my way of avoiding a lawsuit!)

Finally, one of the biggest expenses associated with traveling with kids is the need for childcare. Yes, childcare is needed wherever you go. In fact, parents don't ever go on vacation, they simply take care of their children in a different location. Parents may need to hire a babysitter or enroll their children in a kids' club, and the expenses just keep rolling in!

Backpacking is an Option at Any Age

Yes, this is possible with children but you're more likely to get stressed out and worry about the places that you end up in if you have another life to worry about. Things that might not have been on your radar as a childless person – such as the parts of town you venture into or the type of backpacker lodges you end up at – will come to light. It's all about mindset though – but if you're like the 30% [31] of people who normally stress about these things and can be incredibly neurotic, this is not going to be fun for you.

While many people enjoy this type of travel, it is more commonly associated with young people who are still figuring out their life plans. Backpacking can be physically and emotionally demanding, which is why it may be more appealing to those without children. Firstly, backpacking requires a significant amount of physical endurance. Hiking long distances, carrying a heavy backpack, and navigating unfamiliar terrain can take a toll on the body. Parents, especially those with young children, may find it difficult to meet these physical demands due to the responsibilities and physical limitations that come with having a child. You could definitely backpack with ease without your children because of the fact that you're so used to lugging an additional 25 kilograms around on your hip, back, or shoulders. However, trying to do this while simultaneously carrying the same 25 kilograms of tiny tired legs and arms is going to make things a bit more unwieldy.

Moreover, backpacking usually involves staying in budget accommodations such as hostels or camping, which may not be suitable for families with young children. Families with children may prefer more comfortable and expensive accommodations, which can increase the cost of the trip. If you've never been inside a backpacker lodge, try to picture a hostel that is filled with loud, horny, and probably drunk 20-somethings who are there to sow their wild oats, make new friends, and have a time that they will probably only remember by looking at photos.

Backpacking definitely allows for greater flexibility in terms of travel plans. Those without children can plan their trips on a whim and change their plans without having to worry about losing out on a hefty booking deposit. If they don't like the place, they can pick up and leave in the middle of the night. They can walk the streets at 2 AM and laugh the entire way to their new accommodations while they speak of how that is going to make for a crazy memory one day. The emotional highs and lows that come with this type of escapade often involve stepping outside of one's comfort zone and experiencing new and unfamiliar situations. It's difficult enough trying to step out of one's comfort zone with a partner, let alone children, so this is something that is definitely for a select group of people.

If you want to see the world in a slightly more liberated and carefree manner, backpacking should be something on your list of possibilities. Is this something that parents could do? Yes. Is it as enjoyable with children as it is without them? I personally do not believe so. To each their own.

Chapter 8

My Top Tips for Embracing the Childless Lifestyle

It can feel liberating when you first make the decision to adopt a childless lifestyle. You'll be walking around on cloud nine, thinking that there is absolutely nothing that can weigh you down now that you've accepted this decision. However, the doubts can creep up on you if you're not actively working on your self-awareness. This brings us to my first top tip for embracing the childless lifestyle and that is to become painfully self-aware.

Understanding where your own insecurities come from and how this can impact your desire to travel and mingle with other people is important. It will allow you to take a step back and rationalize with yourself before making drastic decisions. Remember that if you've decided to forego having children because you value your freedom, adopting a puppy when your insecurities crop up is going to be stressful and cumbersome. That is the very same commitment that will cost you financially and prevent you from traveling – albeit not as much as a child would.

So, self-awareness is key and you can try various practices such as journaling and mindfulness meditation to assist with this, but I would recommend a therapy session or two to come up with modalities that work for you. I'll handle the research and let the professionals handle the suggestions and potential liability on that one. But self-awareness would be nothing without some semblance of self-love and self-respect. Being able to love and respect yourself as well as this choice that you have made will be vital in the moments when you don't necessarily like yourself, your partner, your job, or your environment. I have to stress that having a baby for the sake of rescuing a relationship or making you happy as a couple is not going to actually make either of you happy. Nobody holds the key to your happiness but you and stressful times (such as having babies) will amplify whatever you're already feeling.

With those 3 self-oriented rungs on the ladder of your life firmly in place, you can begin exploring groups that are dedicated to solo or couple travel activities. Get out there and meet other people that are childless by choice, but try not to feel as though you have to cut out all of your agemates that have decided to settle down and start a family. If you're coupled up, you can be just as much a family with your partner as your friends with children are.

However, to build your confidence in the decision you've made, surround yourself with as many like-minded people as possible – especially in the early years after making your decision. This is a time when people might feel like they can sway you and you may very well be influenceable at this stage. Those like-minded people will be your rocks so that you can weather the storm and transform into a rock too.

*

Traveling is something that adds meaning to my life and I know of many people who feel the same way. We have almost always been explorers. It's in our nature to seek out new lands in order to experience new sights, sounds, and activities. Our souls yearn for new experiences because this, essentially, is how we keep ourselves from falling into a rut of despair. Be sure to have fun with the aforementioned top tips for embracing the childless lifestyle. Add your own flair to them or just add your own tips to the list. The sky is the limit! Be sure to reach up and grab it.

CHAPTER 9 – THE CHILDLESS CUP RUNNETH OVER

T here is enough strife and turmoil in the world to go around at the moment and these are just opportunities for childless individuals to make a difference through charitable giving. If you've heard about elements such as paying it forward and the goodness of giving, you'll know that a surefire way to feel fulfilled is to help others. Human beings get a massive kick out of helping people who are in need and the consensus seems to be that the feeling of giving is better and more long-lasting than the feeling of receiving.

If you've ever questioned your purpose or had doubts about your abilities, spending time with someone in need and offering them your help will cure that right up!

Everything from your self-esteem to the trusted connections that you form with like-minded people in volunteer environments will keep your cup running over. And you know what they say – you can't pour from an empty cup. Continuing to uplift yourself as you uplift others will definitely have a profound impact on your outlook on life for many people who aren't earning above-average salaries, the only way to continue partaking in these activities is to limit their major expenses. Of course, a child is one of those.

Before we continue, I don't want you to think that finances are at the core of every childless person's decision-making process, because they aren't. There are many people with more-than-sufficient finances who still wouldn't have children (even if you offered to double their net worth).

Whether you have a modest savings account or a gargantuan one or even one that only exists in your imagination, giving back from a cup that is already reasonably full is a great way to keep topping it back up. But this doesn't just stop at charitable organizations. It can extend to your nuclear and extended family members as well.

Cool Aunty Vibes

Spoiling one's nieces and nephews has never been so much fun. In a sense, it's like you get to have children and do all of the fun activities with them without any of this "lifelong responsibility" business. There are so many positives to this that I struggled to narrow them down. Nonetheless, I'll give you my best attempt at doing just that.

One of the biggest perks of being the cool aunty is that there are no financial constraints when it comes to buying gifts for nieces and nephews. This allows for the opportunity to spoil them with extravagant presents that their parents may not be able to afford. It's a wonderful feeling to see the joy on their faces when they receive something special. Just be sure that you're doing everything with good intentions. If you're purchasing presents for your nieces and nephews without the consent of their parents or to show off, you're going to cause unnecessary rifts between the children and their parents as well as between you and their parents. Whether they're your siblings or your brothers- and sisters-in-law is irrelevant.

If you're sure that your siblings- or siblings-in-law are comfortable with this type of relationship with their children, then run with it! Take your nieces and nephews on fun outings and provide them with new experiences that their parents may not have the time or resources for. Whether it's a trip to the zoo, a theme park, or a special dinner out, you can create lasting memories with your loved ones. The beauty of this is that you'll be enhancing the village experience for another couple and providing them with a much-needed break. If anything, it's almost as if we've realized that it truly takes a village to raise a child and instead of demanding that villages form around us, we've decided to become the village. You'll also be enriching the lives of your nieces and nephews because science has proven how a variety of healthy relationships work out in the best interest of every child. [32]

Having the opportunity to build a special bond with your nieces and nephews by spending quality time with them is an added perk that doesn't have to cost a dime. This can create a nurturing and supportive relationship that can be beneficial to the children as they grow and navigate their own lives. As a non-parental figure, you can provide a unique perspective and serve as a positive role model. Becoming a solid sounding board and offering guidance as well as support without the pressures and biases that come with being a parent truly is magical. This deepened sense of purpose and joy that is attributed to contributing to the happiness of one's family, while also being able to maintain one's own independence and lifestyle, is something that many aspire to now.

As your bond with your nieces and nephews continues to grow, so too will your bond with your siblings- or siblings-in-law. You'll develop a newfound appreciation for one another and provide each other with sneak peek experiences into the lives that you both opted not to have.

It is so rewarding to know that one's efforts are valued and appreciated by those around them.

Enriching Family Member's Lives

You don't have to create a family of your own in order to be a part of a family. There is no rule that states that when a woman is of a certain age, she needs to abandon her birth family and go out into the world to create her own. There is still a great amount of joy to be had with the nuclear and extended family that you were born into. Taking care of your parents or helping others in your family to further their studies or start businesses of their own can be tremendously fulfilling.

As people age, many worry about their financial security in their later years. Retirement can be a substantial concern, especially for those who may not have saved enough to live comfortably without a steady income. In many cultures, it is common for adult children to support their parents in their old age. For childless adults, this can be an opportunity to provide financial support and care for their aging parents.

One of the joys of not having children is the ability to focus on the financial well-being of your parents without worrying about the financial strain of supporting children. Childless adults often have more disposable income, which they can use to support their aging parents with basic expenses, medical bills, and day-to-day tasks. For some childless adults, taking care of their parents is a way of giving back for all the love and care their parents provided throughout their childhood. It's an opportunity to show appreciation for the sacrifices their parents made to raise them and give them a good life.

Taking care of aging parents can also provide emotional benefits. Many adult children feel a sense of obligation to take care of their parents, and this can lead to stress and anxiety. For childless adults, there is often less pressure and guilt associated with taking care of their parents. It can be an opportunity to strengthen the bond between parent and child and to have more control over their care. For parents who may not have other children to rely on, childless adults can step in and ensure that their parents are receiving the care they need. This can involve hiring caregivers or even taking care of them personally if the elderly parents aren't completely incapacitated. This, of course, would require round-the-clock care that a working (and thus financially supportive) adult child could not do. Regardless, being able to provide care for parents in this way can be a full-circle moment for the adult child who is childless.

While we're on the topic of taking care of parents, I want to circle back to the point that your own children might not be able to take care of you when you reach old age. You should not have children just to have a private wet nurse if you become incapacitated in old age. If you cannot afford to help your elderly parents right now, what makes you think your children will be in a better financial position to help you later in your life?

Again, assisting elderly parents financially is not for everyone and it is not a must. If you don't feel the urge to provide for your family in a monetary sense, you're not forced to do so. However, being childless by choice gives you the option to choose.

This, of course, will all boil down to whether or not you have a good relationship with your parents amongst many other factors.

Giving Back to Charity

Giving back to your community or donating your time and funds to charitable organizations is one of the most fulfilling pursuits a human being can ever experience. This is more possible when you don't have to pay for private lessons, piano lessons, tennis lessons, braces, school trips, sports gear, and everything else in between.

Those without children can channel that time and money into causes that they care about, leading to a sense of purpose and fulfillment.

Childless individuals give more because they have more to give. They are more philanthropic because they have more disposable income. Several recent studies have indicated that women without children give more to charity than women with children. Men without children also tend to give more to charity than men with children. Not only do they have cash to spare, but they also have more free time. Raising children can be all-consuming, leaving little time for anything else. Those without children, on the other hand, have more time to devote to volunteer work and other charitable activities. For example, they may be able to serve on the board of a non-profit organization, volunteer at a local shelter or soup kitchen, or participate in fundraising events.

Understanding their sense of responsibility to give back to their communities and knowing that we are all one big family is a great motivator for childless couples. These are often people who don't feel the need to create a nuclear family to embrace and appreciate the meaning of the word "family". Those of us who don't have children know that we have a unique opportunity to make a difference, given our free time and financial resources. This is true even for those of us who aren't automatically rolling in the dough that people think childlessness brings on. We tend to empathize with those around us because we have the time to stop and think about what it must feel like to walk a mile in their shoes.

That won't apply to all childless people. Some people are completely devoid of emotional capacity whether they have the time and silence to reflect or not. They want to help. Some want to do so in the quiet shadows and others want to be remembered for it. This is so much so that childless individuals may also be drawn to philanthropy as a way to create a legacy. Without children to pass on their wealth and possessions to, they may want to ensure that their resources are used for good after they are gone. By donating to charitable causes or starting their own charitable foundations, they can leave a lasting impact on the world. The UK's leading analysts of legacies of the deceased found that childless people make up 55% of all of the legacies contributed to charities. [33]

In addition to these motivations, childless individuals may simply find philanthropy to be personally rewarding. Giving back to others can provide a sense of purpose and fulfillment that is difficult to achieve through other means. It can also help them connect with others who share their values and beliefs.

Pairing Travel & Charity

This has to be one of my favourites and if you haven't already heard about what I'll be sharing with you, I urge you to do some more research on the topic when you're done reading. The concept I want to share with you is known as voluntourism and it involves traveling to remote lands to volunteer.

While voluntourism is open to anyone, childless individuals are particularly well-suited to this type of travel because they have more flexibility in their schedules and can more easily take time off from work to pursue their passions. This means that they can take longer trips and commit to longer-term volunteer projects without worrying about the needs of their children. This flexibility also allows them to volunteer on short notice or during unexpected emergencies, such as natural disasters. The amount of manpower that was needed after the 2004 Indian Ocean earthquake and tsunami or the 2022 Düzce earthquake, for example, was staggering.

Even if you aren't dashing into burning buildings or heading off to help in post-disaster zones, voluntourism still has many benefits for those you interact with. As you learn about new cultures and make meaningful connections with people from different backgrounds, so too do they learn about your culture and forge long-lasting connections with you. Volunteering provides a unique lens through which you can experience a new country because you get to work alongside locals and are immersed in local communities. You travel to a foreign country to make a difference in the lives of others and, by the end of it, the person who has been the most positively impacted is you. The level of personal growth that comes from these experiences is exponential and explosive.

The areas in which you can volunteer are also quite diverse. You can consider the following fields for your first, or next, voluntourism adventure:

- Healthcare.
- Childcare.

- Teaching.
- Environmental conservation.
- Wildlife conservation.
- Research.
- Emergency aid.
- Community building.
- Women's rights and welfare.

Voluntourism also offers childless individuals the chance to contribute to causes that are important to them. By volunteering in these aforementioned areas (or any others, for that matter), volunteers can make a tangible impact on the lives of others and help to make the world a better place. Voluntourism has such a positive impact on the communities and organizations that volunteers work with that it would be hard for any true philanthropist and traveler to pass this opportunity up. Many non-profits and charities rely on the support of volunteers to achieve their missions, and the time and effort of voluntourists can be instrumental in furthering their work. If you want to build skills and gain new experiences, this is the way to go. Depending on the type of volunteering, you can gain skills in areas such as project management, leadership, communication, and cross-cultural understanding. These skills can be useful in both personal and professional contexts and can enhance one's resume as well as career prospects.

Above all else, voluntourism can be a fun and fulfilling way to spend a vacation or travel experience. It is something that leaves an indelible mark on the traveler and a moment in time that won't soon be forgotten. Much like backpacking, the night is when this adventure takes a different shape. Due to the fact that you'll be working so hard during the day, you might want to take up the opportunity to explore the local area, try new foods, party, and meet new people during your downtime. This balance of work and play can create a unique and memorable travel experience that is different from traditional tourism. As I said, this type of travel is possible as a family. You could engage in voluntourism during your child's summer break, but it won't always align with your work or business responsibilities. Plus, you might not have excess funds to do a prolonged trip with the whole family because of all those little expenses that were previously mentioned.

*

If you have more than you need, it's best to build a longer table and not a higher wall. Having a child can often lead to higher walls as wealth needs to be preserved, where possible, to ensure that your child's needs are always satisfactorily met. Being childless and engaging in charitable activities within your circles and outside of them could be seen as the equivalent of building a longer table. This is a table that you might want to consider inviting those in the midst of the motherhood paradox over to.

Chapter 10

CHAPTER 10 – THE MOTHERHOOD PARADOX

T he motherhood (or parenthood) paradox is a curious concept because it seeks to understand why people think that having children will make them happier only for it to take away from the happiness that they already have. This is why it's important not to judge childless people – they've seen through the façade and understood that the level of happiness that they have is more than enough. They're not willing to risk losing that happiness on the off chance that they might be a little bit happier with children in their lives.

Children, as they say, are all joy and no happiness at all. Raising them through difficult times can lead to downward spirals into depression, chronic stress, and a reduced sense of life satisfaction.

But not having children (when it's not a choice) can be just as depressing and stressful as not wanting to have children. Whether there are issues around trust in your relationship, the fear of turning into your narcissistic mother, horrendous in-laws to deal with, or the painful reality of infertility, not being able to have children when you want to can be earth-shattering.

Motherhood and the absence of it when it's not on our terms can be paradoxical in nature – seemingly happy on the surface, but rather demoralizing and saddening beneath the water. If you think about it, the choice of whether to embrace motherhood or childlessness and the subsequent lifestyle choices that go along with said decision can be likened to a Mallard. It's all calm and collected on the surface, but in the water below, it's paddling furiously.

That, I imagine, is what the impact of infertility is like.

The Toll of Infertility

The emotional and psychological toll that infertility has on people and the impact that infertility has on relationships should be enough to deter anyone from ever judging a person, or couple, for not having children by a certain age (or ever). This insane pressure to pursue parenthood at all costs leaves people struggling and feeling like they are lost and alone in a world full of people that just don't understand them.

As mentioned earlier, 1 in 6 people will struggle with infertility, which can be brought on by a number of various factors. These can include issues with ovulation and blocked fallopian tubes, polycystic ovarian syndrome (PCOS), and issues with the uterus or cervix. In male partners, infertility could be due to

The emotional toll of infertility can be overwhelming. Women who are struggling with infertility may experience a range of emotions, including anger, sadness, frustration, and guilt. They may feel like they are failing as a woman or a partner and this is with no small thanks to the societal pressure that is placed on women to have children. We need to do away with this idea that women are somehow less whole and less worthy of their existence if they can't have children. In most regions, marrying a woman off against her will is now illegal and punishable by law. Selling daughters off to kings, elders, and village chiefs is a thing of the past in many nations. However, we still carry on the tradition of wanting women to prove their worth to their birth families and their spouses by producing an *heir*. I mean, what is this – The Handmaid's Tale?

We are more than just our uteruses and it's high-time people kept their opinions to themselves.

The feelings of inadequacy and self-doubt that are poured into the cups of young girls and, subsequently, young women are deplorable. The emotional impact of infertility can be particularly challenging for women who have always imagined themselves as mothers and who have built their identities around that idea. For the young woman who has always dreamt of carrying her own child, having a baby shower, and maybe a gender reveal party, as well as all of the precious moments during and after birth, infertility can feel like the world is ending.

For her, the world as she knows it might actually be ending because infertility can also put a significant strain on the relationship with her spouse. Couples who are struggling to conceive may find themselves arguing more often and may feel disconnected from each other. The stress of infertility can also impact sexual intimacy as couples may feel pressure to have sex at certain times or may find that sex has become a chore rather than a source of pleasure. Removing the passion and excitement that comes with spontaneous lovemaking can be the final nail in the coffin for some relationships.

Add to this is the fact that women who are undergoing fertility treatments often experience physical side effects and it's easy to see why they wouldn't ever feel comfortable with, or happy about, discussing their fertility. Having to recollect the in-the-moment or post-procedure discomfort of certain procedures such as egg retrievals and hormone shots is understandably distressing. Not to mention the financial burden that all of this can quickly become. Fertility treatments can cost anywhere from €9,000 to €23,000 [34] and most medical insurance does not cover these types of procedures. Not to be insensitive here, but if medical insurers don't see fertility and procreation as an absolute essential, who does your family think they are to push that agenda on you?

Having to make difficult decisions about how much money you are willing to spend on treatment and, potentially, taking on additional debt can cause major upheavals in your life. This can lead to decisions to delay other financial goals in order to pay for these treatments and, by the time you have a child (if you're one of the fortunate women), you might be starting a family on very shaky financial ground. One of the key ways that most experts suggest dealing with this stress is to seek support from friends, family, or a therapist who specializes in infertility issues. Talking to someone who understands what you are going through can be incredibly helpful and can provide a much-needed sense of validation and support. If you don't have anyone to turn to because of the fact that everyone you thought was on your team turned out to be more concerned with you popping out a child than your well-being, then this is going to be difficult to attain.

If you've ever struggled with depression, this is going to be a tough time for you to navigate because you may find yourself slipping back into a state of depression. You might just find it increasingly difficult to take care of yourself both physically and emotionally. Having an accountability partner that is both loving and supportive can get you through these times if your spouse is going through a difficult time and unable to uplift you. They can help you stay on track with your self-care and this may involve taking time to do things that you enjoy. Included in some of the more common ways to engage in self-care are exercise, reading, or spending time in nature. You could also consider exploring alternative treatments such as acupuncture, massage, or meditation, which can help to reduce stress and promote relaxation. If anything, doing things that you wouldn't normally do can be a welcome break from the depressing mundanity that you've been going through.

Whatever you need to do to mentally detach from some of the hurtful questions and comments that you might receive as a person struggling with fertility, do that. You deserve every ounce of comfort you can get.

Surrogacy Being Pushed Over Adoption

This is one of the unwittingly hurtful areas of infertility that people tiptoe into. Asking a couple whether they would consider surrogacy or adoption is like the modern-day version of asking people when they plan on having children. It can be totally harmless in the eyes of the person asking the question but, depending on the nature of the relationship and the mental status of the person that they're asking, this might not go down so well. Maybe a couple wants the experience of carrying their own child. Maybe they don't want some random person carrying their child. Maybe they do. Maybe they would rather adopt but are worried that their family wouldn't accept the adopted child. There are so many factors that come into play when a couple wants a child and is childless, but not by choice.

One of the main reasons why some couples may not want to use a surrogate or adopt is the desire to have a biological child. For many people, the idea of passing on their genes and creating a child that is a product of their love and commitment is an important aspect of parenthood. Surrogacy and adoption, while noble options, do not provide the same genetic connection and may not fulfill this desire. Additionally, surrogacy and adoption can be expensive and time-consuming processes. Many couples may not have the financial resources to pursue these options, and the prospect of years of legal and bureaucratic red tape can be daunting.

Surrogacy is often the quicker option for couples wanting to have a child – especially if they want a child of their own – but it is also the more expensive option. Not only is there egg and sperm retrieval involved but there is also the insemination of the surrogate. Unless you conduct this process via a credible agency, you could find yourself in a situation whereby the surrogate tries to extort you by holding your unborn child "hostage" in her belly. If you're wondering how she could possibly do that, here's a fun fact for you. Until your surrogate gives birth and sings your baby's rights over to you, she is legally the mother of your child and has full control over her body and birthing outcomes. The finer details of these technicalities will vary from country to country and, in some cases, from state to state, but this is something that often puts couples off of this possibility. Also, the wait to be matched with a child or surrogate can be agonizing, and the uncertainty of the outcome can be a constant source of stress.

If that isn't enough to deter them, their cultural backgrounds might be. In some cultures, the stigma or shame around not being able to conceive naturally is too much for couples to bear. They feel indebted to their families as well as the beliefs that they were raised with and they may worry about how others will perceive them if they pursue adoption or surrogacy. This pressure can be overwhelming and can lead some couples to avoid these options altogether. Some religions or cultures may view surrogacy or adoption as unnatural or even immoral, and adhering to these beliefs may prevent some couples from pursuing these options. Elders in these contexts can be quite toxic and narcissistic, making couples question whether going through all of that strain to bring a child into the family would even be worth it in the end.

The Narcissistic Mother (or Parent)

We already know what it's like to deal with the judgment from family and friends (and society in general) because we've explored this at length in previous chapters. However, one thing we haven't considered is the person who was born to toxic, narcissistic, or otherwise abusive parents. There are grown women – mothers to boot – who control their daughters and make them feel like they owe them a grandchild.

A narcissistic or abusive mother is a parent who puts her own needs and desires above those of her children, often using manipulation, guilt, or fear to control them. This kind of mother is often emotionally distant, critical, and volatile, creating an unstable and unpredictable environment for her children to grow up in. For daughters of narcissistic or abusive mothers, the decision to not have children of their own can be a way of breaking the cycle of abuse and protecting their own mental health. Women who grew up with a narcissistic or abusive mother often struggle with unresolved trauma and feelings of anger. These negative emotions can impact their ability to parent and lead to unintentionally repeating the same parenting patterns they experienced as a child.

Many daughters fear that they will become like their mothers, perpetuating the cycle of abuse and neglect.

Furthermore, growing up with a narcissistic or abusive mother can create a deep sense of distrust towards others, making it challenging for daughters to form close relationships. This difficulty in trusting others can extend to potential partners and future children, making it challenging for daughters to envision having a family of their own.

In this paradox, the daughter of a narcissistic or abusive mother often chooses to prioritize her own mental health and self-care, essentially breaking the cycle of abuse by never having children of her own. If she has to be the first one in her family to set healthy boundaries, seek therapy, and avoid situations that trigger negative emotions, that is what she will do. Moreover, as she becomes more self-aware, she will most likely realize that having children would interfere with her ability to prioritize her own well-being and could potentially trigger unresolved trauma.

This is not a risk that woman on her path to healing is willing to take.

The Parent Trap

You could have everything you need to conceive and raise a healthy child – perfect fertility, accepting and kind parents, wonderful siblings and friends, and a spouse from heaven. However, if you have in-laws from hell, you're still going to have an issue (or several) to deal with. If you have unkind in-laws that would ruin the pregnancy experience or that would manipulate the situation, this might make you feel torn between having a child and not wanting to cut off certain family members that you know will be toxic to your partner, your baby, your journey, and the upbringing of your child.

Having a partner with intrusive or controlling parents can be a challenging experience, especially for women who are considering starting a family. The constant interference, criticism, and demands from in-laws can cause immense stress and strain on a relationship. For some women, this can lead to the decision not to have children, as they fear that their in-laws will exert the same level of control over their parenting decisions. For some reason, there seems to be some type of universal law that the parents who are controlling, retired, and have far too much time on their hands are the ones that live closest to you and your spouse. As such, they're often a couple's only choice of affordable or emergency childcare when they absolutely have to nip off without their child and their sitter is unavailable. This can lead to power struggles between parents and grandparents as these types of grandparents will always feel that they know what's best. The fear of losing control over their own lives is enough to make most women head for the hills and prevent pregnancy at all costs. To have to deal with controlling in-laws who often feel second-guess or overrule a woman's decisions can leave her feeling powerless and frustrated. These feelings of powerlessness can be magnified when it comes to parenting decisions, as in-laws may feel entitled to provide unsolicited advice or even try to take control of important decisions such as the child's education, religious upbringing, circumcision (where boys are concerned), when to start solids, how many naps the baby should have, how plump they should be by a certain age, and even the child's overall medical care.

For some women, the pressure from in-laws to have children can also be a significant factor in their decision not to have children.

In-laws may put pressure on their children to have children, often with the expectation that they will provide grandchildren to carry on the family name or legacy. This pressure can be especially intense if the couple has been married for a long time or if the in-laws are experiencing health issues that make them worry about not being able to see their grandchildren. However, this pressure can also cause resentment and frustration, leading women to feel like they are not in control of their own reproductive decisions. What worsens this is if the child of said controlling parents – or spouse – does not step in to handle their parents, this will lead to a fallout in the marriage. What's so strange is that many of these controlling in-laws couldn't fathom being controlled by their own in-laws and they either never experienced this or they did and:

a. They feel like it's their turn to control someone else's grown child.
b. They think that this is the norm and actually, delusionally, thank their in-laws for putting them through the wringer when they were younger.

Another reason why women may choose not to have children when dealing with intrusive or controlling in-laws is the fear of creating a rift in the family. Women who have controlling in-laws may worry that their decision to have children will cause tension or conflict in the family, leading to a breakdown in relationships. This can be a challenging situation, especially if the in-laws are an important part of the family or if they have a significant influence on the couple's social or professional lives.

In addition to these concerns, women who have intrusive or controlling in-laws may also worry about the impact that these relationships will have on their children. In-laws who exert control or interfere with parenting decisions can create a stressful and unstable environment for children, leading to negative outcomes such as behavioral problems, anxiety, or depression. Their presence in their grandchildren's lives can also cause those very grandchildren to disrespect their parents in the name of "only listening to their grandparents". On the other hand, women who have experienced this type of behavior from their in-laws may worry that their children will also be subjected to this type of treatment.

Despite these concerns, there are ways in which women can navigate the challenges of having intrusive or controlling in-laws and still have children if they choose to do so. The key is to establish clear boundaries and communicate openly with in-laws about expectations and decisions. This can be a challenging process, as in-laws may be resistant to change or feel like their opinions are not being respected. However, by being firm and consistent in setting boundaries and communicating their needs and expectations, women can create a stable and supportive environment for their families. Just keep in mind that some elderly people are like big children themselves. They might stop speaking to you and constantly call their child to complain about how they don't see you or the children in spite of their decisions. They act like spoiled children who have nothing better to do than complain and prioritize their relationship with their child at the expense of their child having a healthy relationship with their spouse.

If this sounds like a parent trap that you're all too familiar with, I can completely understand why having children might not be a choice that you're open to making.

Even if you want to have children in spite of these factors, you may find yourself in a situation where your in-laws hold delayed conception and even infertility over your head. It might all become too much to deal with, leading you to cut them off for good, and rightfully so. That should be regarded as a form of bullying and abuse.

*

The motherhood paradox is one that has been the bane of women's lives for far too long. For women who struggle with infertility, this can be cripplingly detrimental to their mental health. It's bad enough to experience feelings of inadequacy and hopelessness, but for it to be spurred on by society is uncalled-for and borderline emotional abuse.

Now that you have wrapped up the final chapter of this guide to being childless by choice, let's recap some of the most featured topics that seem to apply to this choice across a variety of personal areas of life. That's up next.

IN CLOSING

As we come to the end of this book, it's clear that there are many joys and benefits to being childless by choice. Whether it's the freedom to pursue a career, travel the world, or simply have more time for self-care and personal pursuits, there are countless ways in which not having children can enrich our lives.

Of course, choosing not to have children is not without its challenges. Society places a great deal of pressure on individuals and couples to have children, and it can be difficult to navigate these expectations and come to terms with the decision to opt out of parenthood. Additionally, infertility and other reproductive issues can be a painful and difficult experience for those who do want children but are unable to conceive.

But despite these challenges, the benefits of being childless are clear. Not only do childless individuals and couples have more time and flexibility, they also have the opportunity to live a life of purpose and passion, pursuing their own interests and goals without the constraints of raising a family.

One of the greatest joys of being childless is the freedom to explore our own identities and find our true purpose in life. Without the responsibilities of parenthood, we have the time and energy to devote to our passions and interests, whether that means pursuing a new career, starting a business, or devoting ourselves to a cause that we believe in.

In addition to allowing us to pursue our own interests, being childless can also have a positive impact on our relationships with others. Without the demands of raising children, we are free to invest more time and energy into our friendships, romantic relationships, and other important connections. We can travel, explore new places and cultures, and enjoy experiences that might not be possible with children in tow.

And while it's true that not having children can sometimes result in feelings of loneliness or isolation, it's important to remember that there are many other ways to build meaningful connections with others. Whether it's through volunteering, joining clubs or groups, or simply reaching out to friends and family, there are countless opportunities to find community and connection outside of parenthood.

Ultimately, the decision to have or not have children is deeply personal, and there is no one "right" choice for everyone. But for those who do choose to live a childless life, the benefits and joys are plentiful. From the freedom to pursue our own interests and passions to the opportunity to build deep and meaningful connections with others, being childless offers a unique and fulfilling way to live our lives.

So as we close the book on this exploration of the joys of being childless by choice, let us remember that the decision to live a childless life is not one to be taken lightly. But for those who make this choice, the rewards are great, and the possibilities are endless.

Thank you for reading.

REFERENCES & CITATIONS

1. Boyd, R., & Richerson, P. J. (2009). ***Culture and the evolution of human cooperation.*** Philosophical transactions of the Royal Society of London. Series B, Biological sciences, 364(1533), 3281–3288. https://doi.org/10.1098/rstb.2009.0134

2. Martin Sikora et al., (2017). ***Ancient genomes show social and reproductive behavior of early Upper Paleolithic foragers.*** Science358,659-662. DOI:10.1126/science.aao1807

3. Beddington, E. (2016). ***Why your teenager thinks you're an idiot.*** The Guardian. https://www.theguardian.com/lifeandstyle/2016/jun/25/why-your-teenager-thinks-youre-an-idiot

4. UNICEF. (2023). ***How Many?*** UNICEF. https://data.unicef.org/how-many/

5. Beck, C. T., Watson, S., & Gable, R. K. (2018). ***Traumatic Childbirth and Its Aftermath: Is There Anything Positive?*** The Journal of perinatal education, 27(3), 175-184. https://doi.org/10.1891/1058-1243.27.3.175

6. Gibbons, S. (2017). ***8 Reasons Why Millennials Are More Productive than Any Other Generation.*** Entrepreneur. https://www.entrepreneur.com/business-news/8-reasons-why-millennials-are-more-productive-than-any/305794

7. Dias, F. A., Chance, J., & Buchanan, A. (2020). ***The motherhood penalty and The fatherhood premium in employment during covid-19: evidence from The united states.*** Research in social

stratification and mobility, 69, 100542.
https://doi.org/10.1016/j.rssm.2020.100542

8. WHO Blog Team. (2023). ***1 in 6 people globally affected by infertility: WHO.*** https://www.who.int/news/item/04-04-2023-1-in-6-people-globally-affected-by-infertility#:~:text=Around%2017.5%25%20of%20the%20adult, care%20for%20those%20in%20need.

9. McKenna, J. (2018). ***Here's why Sweden is the best country to be a parent.*** WEF. https://www.weforum.org/agenda/2018/01/this-is-why-sweden-is-one-of-the-best-countries-in-the-world-to-be-a-parent/#:~:text=The%20country%20was%20last%20year,the%20Netherlands%20for%20family%20living.&text=Sweden's%20parents%20are%20given%20more,those%20in%20any%20other%20country.

10. Velkoff, V., et al. (2014). ***U.S. Population Will Get Older but Remain Younger than Most Developed Countries.*** United States Census Bureau. https://www.census.gov/newsroom/blogs/random-samplings/2014/05/u-s-population-will-get-older-but-remain-younger-than-most-developed-countries.html#:~:text=U.S.%20Population%20Remains%20Younger%20than%20Most%20Developed%20Countries&text=A%20.,organization%20in%20the%20United%20States.

11. Adkuloo, N. (2023). ***How Much Childcare Costs by State in the USA in 2023.*** Illumine. https://illumine.app/blog/how-much-childcare-costs-by-state-in-usa/#:~:text=The%20average%20cost%20of%20childcare%20in%20the%20USA%20is%20%2414760%20annually.

12. Money Helper Team. (2023). ***Average childcare costs.*** Money Helper. https://www.moneyhelper.org.uk/en/family-and-care/becoming-a-parent/childcare-costs

13. The Local Team. (2022). ***How does the cost of childcare in Sweden compare to other countries?*** The Local. https://www.thelocal.se/20220927/how-does-the-cost-of-childcare-in-sweden-compare-to-other-countries#:~:text=Preschool%20childcare%20is%20not%20free,month%20(fees%20for%202022).

14. Huggies Team. (2023). ***Child care cost.*** Huggies. https://www.huggies.co.za/articles/pregnancy/parenting/child-care-cost

15. Iyer, S. (2023). ***The Cost Of Education And Childcare In Australia.*** Expat Network. https://expatnetwork.com/the-cost-of-education-and-childcare-in-australia/

16. Budiman, A. (2020). ***Key findings about U.S. immigrants.*** Pew Research Center. https://www.pewresearch.org/short-reads/2020/08/20/key-findings-about-u-s-immigrants/#:~:text=The%20United%20States%20has%20more,fifth%20of%20the%20world's%20migrants.

17. Bove, T. (2022). ***Adults are living with their parents at unprecedented levels as crushing debt, a runaway housing market, and the pandemic make independence impossible.*** Fortune. https://fortune.com/2022/03/25/more-adults-living-with-parents-than-ever-pew-research-pandemic-covid-great-depression/

18. Rivelli, E. (2023). ***How Much Does It Cost To Have A Baby? 2023 Averages.*** Forbes. https://www.forbes.com/advisor/health-insurance/average-childbirth-cost/

19. upGrad Abroad Team. (2023). ***Bachelor Degree Cost in USA - Tuition Fees & Cost of Living.*** upGrad Abroad. https://www.upgradabroad.com/articles/cost-of-bachelor-degree-in-usa/

20. Noack, R. (2015). ***Why Danish students are paid to go to college.*** The Washington Post. https://www.washingtonpost.com/news/worldviews/wp/2015/02/04/why-danish-students-are-paid-to-go-to-college/

21. Adamczyk, A. (2019). ***Most Americans think young adults should be financially independent by 22–but only 24% are.*** CNBC. https://www.cnbc.com/2019/10/26/only-24percent-of-young-adults-are-financially-independent-by-22-per-pew.html

22. Mughal S, et al. (2022). ***Postpartum Depression.*** StatPearls Publishing. https://www.ncbi.nlm.nih.gov/books/NBK519070/

23. Aggarwal, N. (2020). ***Parents Make 1,750 Tough Decisions in Baby's First Year, Survey Says.*** The Bump. https://www.thebump.com/news/tough-parenting-decisions-first-year-baby-life

24. Becker, C., et al. (2019). ***Marriage, parenthood and social network: Subjective well-being and mental health in old age.*** PLOS One Open Access Research. https://journals.plos.org/plosone/article/metrics?id=10.1371/journal.pone.0218704#citedHeader

25. The Nordstjernan Team. (2020). ***The cost of children.*** Nordstjernan. https://nordstjernan.com/news/education%7Cresearch/5783/#:~:text=Well%2C%20in%20Sweden%2C%20it%20costs,until%20his%20or%20her18th%20birthday.

26. The Mint Team. (2022). ***How Much Does it Cost To Raise a Child in 2022? Things for Prospective Parents To Consider.***

Intuit Mint Life. https://mint.intuit.com/blog/planning/how-much-does-it-cost-to-raise-a-child/#:~:text=As%20they%20grow%20up%2C%20you,region%20and%20household%20income%20level.

27. Ramaswamy, C. (2019). It is a scandal that working mothers are 40% more stressed than other people. The Guardian. https://www.theguardian.com/lifeandstyle/2019/jan/28/scandal-working-mothers-40-per-cent-more-stressed-other-people

28. Paul, A. (2023). *What are the Consequences of Social Isolation in the Remote Workspace?* Open Growth. https://www.opengrowth.com/resources/what-are-the-consequences-of-social-isolation-in-the-remote-workspace#:~:text=Effects%20on%20Mental%20Health&text=One%20study%20found%20that%20those,and%20increased%20feelings%20of%20stress.

29. Mwanza, E. (2022). *Money and Me: Does Having Kids Mean Death to My Dreams?* Money254. https://www.money254.co.ke/post/money-and-me-does-having-kids-mean-death-to-my-dreams-money-and-me

30. Chopik, W. (2017). *Associations among relational values, support, health, and well-being across the adult lifespan.* Wiley Online Library – Journal of Personal Relationships. https://doi.org/10.1111/pere.12187

31. Chamorro-Premuzic, T. (2022). *Are Successful People More Neurotic?* Forbes. https://www.forbes.com/sites/tomaspremuzic/2022/06/07/are-successful-people-more-neurotic/?sh=52f3d1a85860

32. NSPCC Learning. (2021). *Healthy and unhealthy relationships.* NSPCC. https://learning.nspcc.org.uk/safeguarding-child-protection/healthy-and-unhealthy-relationships#:~:text=Forming%20healthy%2C%20positive%20

relationships%20helps,to%20make%20their%20own%20decisi
ons.

33. Barber, M. (2019). ***Childless adults make huge impact with charitable donations.*** Toronto Star.
https://www.thestar.com/opinion/contributors/2019/06/16/chil
dless-adults-make-huge-impact-with-charitable-
donations.html?rf

34. Gurevich, R. RN. (2022). ***How Much Does IVF Really Cost?***
Very Well Family. https://www.verywellfamily.com/how-
much-does-ivf-cost-
1960212#:~:text=If%20you%20include%20all%20the,expensive
%20of%20the%20donor%20options.

Printed in Great Britain
by Amazon

27745496R10088